Communication Skills for Children's Nurses

Edited by

Veronica Lambert
Tony Long
Deirdre Kelleher

Mc Graw Hill Open University Press

Open University Press
McGraw-Hill Education
McGraw-Hill House
Shoppenhangers Road
Maidenhead
Berkshire
England
SL6 2QL

email: enquiries@openup.co.uk
world wide web: www.openup.co.uk

and Two Penn Plaza, New York, NY 10121-2289, USA

First published 2012

A catalogue record of this book is available from the British Library

ISBN-13: 978-0-33-524286-3
ISBN-10: 0-33-524286-3
e-ISBN: 978-0-33-524288-7

Library of Congress Cataloging-in-Publication Data
CIP data applied for

Typeset by Aptara Inc., India
Printed and bound by CPI Group (UK) Ltd, Croydon, CR0 4YY

Fictitious names of companies, products, people, characters and/or data that may be used herein (in case studies or in examples) are not intended to represent any real individual, company, product or event.

The **McGraw·Hill** Companies

Praise for this book

Contents

Tables and figures

Editors and contributors

The editors

Veronica Lambert is a lecturer in nursing at the School of Nursing and Human Sciences, Dublin City University. She is a registered general and children's nurse and completed her BNS (Hons) degree and PhD at Trinity College Dublin. The voice of children is central to Veronica's research, which is underpinned by the concepts of communication (among health professionals, children, parents, families, peers, and the community), child and family psychosocial healthcare needs, the humanistic side of technology, the use of creative/performance arts in health care and creative participatory media to engage with children in research.

Tony Long is professor of child and family health in the University of Salford School of Nursing, Midwifery and Social Work. He leads CYP@Salford, a multi-professional children and families research centre, in which there are research programmes for the evaluation of the impact of health and social care services for children and families, supporting parental coping with children with enduring problems, and improving quality of life outcomes for children after acquired brain injury. He is Visiting Professor at Liverpool John Moores University, working with the children and young people research group.

Deirdre Kelleher is a lecturer at University College Dublin. She is undertaking a PhD to investigate fathers' experiences of caring for children with complex needs. Deidre has a particular interest in child development and legislative and policy aspects relating to the needs of children and their families. This has been further enhanced by her role as a board member of the Irish charity Children in Hospital Ireland, which works directly with children in hospital to help them cope with illness and hospitalization, and provides on-going support to fathers and mothers.

The contributors

Stacey Atkinson is a senior nurse lecturer and route leader for the BSc (Hons) learning disability nursing programme at the University of Huddersfield. Stacey qualified as a learning disability nurse in 1987 and worked as a community nurse with both adults and children with learning disabilities. Her particular areas of interest include meeting the behavioural, sexuality, and emotional needs of children with learning disabilities, and communication forms a large part of each of these areas. She studied the communication needs of children with learning disabilities during her primary degree and as part of her master's in healthcare ethics and law. She also developed a sexual education programme for children with severe learning disabilities for which she received nursing awards and an MBE.

Frances Binns is the therapeutic and specialized play consultant and professional lead at the Royal Manchester Children's Hospital and the North West Play Healthcare Network and Benchmarking Team. With 34 years' experience, she has developed therapeutic and specialized play in hospitals and other healthcare establishments for children and young people from birth to 19 years, promoting inclusivity, equality, and diversity at a strategic level. She has received NHS and third sector awards for achievements, and was made a Pioneer of the Nation by the Queen for her needle-phobia play referral service work. Her current work includes developing quality service improvements for children and young people with autism or complex needs when accessing hospital services.

Debbie Fallon is a lecturer/researcher at the University of Manchester. She has been registered as a general and sick children's nurse, and as a nurse educator, for over twenty years. She completed her PhD in sociology at Goldsmiths, University of London. Her research interests and publications focus on the health and wellbeing of young people, and their meaningful participation in research. Debbie has been a trustee at Brook Manchester, the Association of Young People's Health, and she is the nurse academic representative on the Royal College of General Practitioners Adolescent Interest Group.

Nóirín Hayes is a developmental psychologist and researcher with a particular interest in early childhood education, children's rights, and policy formation and implementation. She is a founder member of the Children's Rights Alliance and the Centre for Social and Educational Research (CSER) at the Dublin Institute of Technology. She is professor emeritus at the CSER where she leads a number of research projects in the field of early childhood and is research supervisor to a group of PhD students. She is the author of a number of books, reports, and research articles on practice and policy in early childhood education, children's rights, and childhood.

Paula Hicks is a senior researcher at Trinity College Dublin. Paula has designed and delivered modules in the area of health informatics at undergraduate and postgraduate level. Her expertise is in the use of innovative technology solutions and interventions (such as online communities, social media, and web 2.0) to support improved psychosocial outcomes for children in hospital, leading to two award-winning projects: Áit Eile (eEurope Award for eHealth 2004) and Solas (Irish Healthcare Awards 2008 and Astellas Changing Tomorrow Award for Innovation 2010). She has published extensively in the area of health informatics. She holds an MSc in health informatics and is a member of the Health Informatics Society of Ireland (HISI) and Irish Computer Society (ICS).

Philomena Keogh is a lecturer in social and educational studies in the Dublin Institute of Technology. She is involved in developing and facilitating various degree programmes at undergraduate and masters level. Previous to her current appointment she was a registered general and children's nurse with many years of experience working in nurse education in a large children's hospital. She has worked with a consultancy firm providing skills training for people employed in the public services sector. She has authored a wide range of articles and one book.

Ursula Kilkelly is a professor of law at University College Cork (UCC) where she teaches child law and children's rights on UCC's graduate law programmes. Ursula is a widely published children's rights scholar and author of *The Child and the European Convention on Human Rights* (1999, 2nd edition forthcoming) and *Children's Rights in Ireland: Law, Policy and Practice* (2008). She has undertaken a number of research projects on children's rights to health care, including a study of children's right to be heard in the healthcare setting (with M. Donnelly), published by the Office of the Minister for Children in 2007, another with the Council of Europe on children's experience of health care, and an ongoing project with the Ombudsman for Children (with E. Savage and J. Hourihane) commissioned in 2011.

Philip Larkin trained as a registered nurse and children's nurse in the UK and worked in paediatric oncology and bone marrow transplantation. He subsequently trained as a health visitor and district nurse in London and worked in community paediatrics, before moving to palliative care in 1990. Phil holds a PhD from the Catholic University of Louvain, Belgium, a master's in health professional education from the University of Huddersfield, and a BSc in community nursing from Kings College London. He is director of the Masters in Palliative Care programme and leads on the education strand in relation to caring for children and families with life-limiting illness. He has published extensively on issues relative to palliative care, palliative care nursing and education. In 2007, Phil received the Lifetime Achievement Award by Macmillan Cancer Support and the International Journal of Palliative Nursing in recognition of his European and international work for palliative nursing education.

Joan Livesley is a senior lecturer in children's and young people's nursing and research, and has published in the fields of children in hospital, multi-agency working for children's services, and evidence-based practice. A registered children's nurse, she undertakes research in partnership with children and young people in health and social care settings, in institutions, and in the community. She leads a research programme in children's and young people's nursing, professional roles, and practice development. She has a clinical background in services for children in hospital, including intensive care and renal replacement, and currently links with NHS community services.

Emer Murphy received her bachelor's degree in psychiatric nursing from University College Dublin in 2006 and completed her postgraduate diploma in child and adolescent mental health nursing at the National University of Ireland Galway in 2009. She has received accolades for her academic achievement both at undergraduate and postgraduate level. Emer is currently in the process of achieving a qualification in humanistic and integrative psychotherapy. She has experience of working with children and adolescents as outpatients, day patients, and inpatients.

Her areas of professional interest include group facilitation and working with families.

Colman Noctor is a nurse therapist at St. Patrick's University Hospital, Dublin. He has over 15 years of international experience in the area of child and adolescent mental health. Colman specializes in psychoanalytical psychotherapy with children and adolescents. He received a master's in child and adolescent psychoanalytical psychotherapy in 2008 and he is a registered psychoanalytic psychotherapist and currently applying to become an advanced nurse practitioner in child and adolescent mental health. Colman has a special interest in eating disorders and paediatric liaison work and has experience of inpatient, day hospital, and community settings. Colman is also an adjunct lecturer in University College Dublin.

Eileen Savage is a professor of nursing at the School of Nursing and Midwifery, University College Cork. She researches chronic illness management in children and adolescents with a specific interest in self and family management, including how healthcare interventions and practices can be tailored to accommodate their views on how best to meet their needs. She has been a visiting professor at the School of Nursing, Yale University, New Haven, CT, undertaking research at the Self and Family Management Centre for Vulnerable Populations. She has undertaken a number of funded studies and has published on chronic illness management. She is a member of the editorial board of *Chronic Illness*.

Joanna Smith is lecturer in children and young people's nursing at the School of Nursing, Midwifery and Social Work, University of Salford, Greater Manchester. She is a registered general and sick children's nurse and has over 15 years' experience nursing children with complex needs including neurological conditions. Joanna has worked in higher education for the last twelve years and completed her PhD at the University of Leeds in 2011. Her main research interests relate to parent–professional engagement and collaboration in the context of children with long-term conditions.

Victoria Stewart is the development officer at the *Early Break* Young People and Families Drug and Alcohol Service. With a BA (Hons) in social ethics, and having worked in teaching and substance misuse roles in a young offenders' institution, she has many years of experience in the voluntary sector supporting families affected by parental substance-misuse. Currently leading on the development of the award-winning Holding Families Service, Victoria has presented at international conferences on the excellent outcomes of the service and on the effects of parental substance-misuse on children. While offering consultancy to services, she has developed training on parental substance-misuse and is a member of the local Children's Safeguarding Board training pool.

Janet Wray is a nurse consultant for children, young people, and families working in community services for Pennine Care NHS Foundation Trust. After registration in adult and paediatric nursing, with experience in an accident and emergency environment, Janet completed the health visitor BSc programme and subsequently the advanced practitioner MSc programme. Having a strong commitment to the development of children's community services, particularly with vulnerable families, Janet's current position utilizes strategic leadership and clinical expertise to influence community service redesign. Her clinical skills are drawn upon in the assessment and management of children with neuro-developmental disability, including autistic spectrum disorders, developmental coordination disorder, and attention deficit hyperactivity disorder.

Foreword

When there is a job to be done, often in a challenging and pressured environment, it is easy to overlook the importance of communication. At first glance, when considering clinical priorities in a paediatric setting, it does not appear to be the most important part of a nurse's duties, as there is so much to do with limited time.

It is, however, central to the experience of the child or young person being cared for. Communication, in often small and simple ways, is central to building a rapport with children and gaining their trust; it is also key to offering assurance to a naturally concerned family, making them feel valued and part of the process.

In my thirty years working with children, I have seen examples of great practice, where professionals charged with the care of children have listened respectfully and empathetically, where they have communicated sensitively and skilfully, and where they have gone to extraordinary efforts to support a child even in the most difficult of circumstances. I have also seen examples where there has been no attempt to communicate appropriately with children, where their views have not been sought, and where there is consequently very little trust on the part of the young person. The examples in the second category are not necessarily cases of professionals who choose not to communicate, but sometimes in developing as professionals they may not have placed a value on communication, perhaps having not considered it to be of great importance.

It strikes me that the first element of addressing this is ensuring that professionals are aware of the importance of communication. The second is to realize that it is not just an innate ability; communication is a skill that can and should be refined over time. This is not necessarily an easy thing to do. It is undeniable that certain aspects of communicating with children and young people can be challenging, even more so when they are unwell and frightened. I know that it is not easy all of the time – when engaging with very young children or children for whom non-verbal communication is important – approaching the issue of children's evolving capacities and the role of parents and guardians, and handling the cultural sensitivities of children from diverse backgrounds.

From my work as Ombudsman for Children, it has become clear that learning to communicate and hearing what children have to say is an essential part of a wider transformation of the public service *vis-à-vis* children. This is, to my mind, a fundamental building block in a culture of respect for children's rights.

My conviction is rooted in Article 12 of the United Nations Convention on the Rights of the Child, which requires states to assure to children capable of forming their own views the right to express those views freely in all matters affecting them, with due weight given to those views in accordance with the age and maturity of the child. This principle – a principle that has an elevated status in the framework of the UN Convention because of its cross-cutting nature – underpins all of the work of my Office and is one that I actively promote in my engagement with public bodies.

The language of human rights, evoking as it does a legal conception of states' obligations to its citizens, can sometimes seem distant from the realities of professionals such as nurses who work with children on a daily basis. But their work is at the heart of vindicating children's rights. It is precisely in everyday circumstances that children encounter justice – and indeed injustice – be it in schools, hospitals or in the community. And it is those who work to ensure that we do right by children in all those different contexts that are the ones protecting their rights.

This brings to mind a question posed by Eleanor Roosevelt, one of the architects of the Universal Declaration of Human Rights. She was once asked where universal human rights begin. Her answer was that they begin in small places, close to home – so close and so small that they cannot be seen on any maps of the world. Yet they are the world of the individual person.

An essential part of advancing children's rights is ensuring that they feel respected and listened to – in short, that they matter. This is the crucial role played by communication and this is why it is so important that all professionals working with and for children have the skills to ensure that young people have this experience of respect.

The publication of *Communication Skills for Children's Nurses* is therefore a very welcome development. It is a rich and stimulating collection that will provide invaluable guidance to children's nurses on this important topic. I commend it to those with an interest in developing their communication skills or in training nurses working with children.

Much of what I have learned personally about communication and children's rights, I learned in the child health environment.

I have no doubt that this book will have a positive impact to nurses' professional development and on children's experience of healthcare settings as a result.

Emily Logan
Republic of Ireland Ombudsman for Children

Theoretical foundations of communication

Veronica Lambert

Communication is an essential feature of health care and one of the main roles you will undertake as a health professional. This textbook will help you to learn the practicalities and theoretical underpinnings of communication skills for engaging with children and their families. Children will be deemed persons under the age of 18 years unless otherwise specified. Alongside defining children according to their number of lived years, their developmental life-course as well as social, cultural, legal, and political contexts will be considered. Families take many forms: 'in essence, the family is who it identifies itself to be, and therefore a family assessment should start by asking the family, who is in this family?' (Hemphill and Dearmun 2006: 19). This chapter sets the scene for the chapters to follow by presenting some theoretical perspectives and principles of communication.

Learning outcomes

By the end of this chapter you should be able to:

1. Describe the core elements and interpersonal skills required to enact effective communication with children and their families
2. Identify and reflect on the personal and situational challenges encountered in engaging in dialogue with children and their families
3. Demonstrate knowledge of various theoretical lenses, or models, through which communication behaviours can be understood

Introduction

Child and family centred care is a central tenet and fundamental principle of providing quality health care to children and families. A core aspect of child and family centred care is that parents are extensively involved in caring for their child; the family is recognized as a constant in the child's life whereas health professionals are involved intermittently (Shelton *et al.* 1987). Quality health care encompasses listening to and involving children in their own care and decision-making processes. Encouraging the active participation of both child and parent(s) in health care is dependent upon your ability to manage the dynamics of a three-way dialogical relationship between yourself, the child, and the parent(s) in the context of a busy healthcare, and/or home, setting.

Triadic interactions

With increased third-party involvement, as in child–parent–health professional engagement, the dynamics of the interaction become increasingly more complex (Gabe *et al.* 2004; Pyorala 2004). In such circumstances, parents often assume an intermediary stance between you and the child. On the one hand, parents might hold a supportive role, acting as a communication buffer for the child, answering difficult questions for the child, empowering the child to take part, and enhancing the child's understanding and memory (Gibson *et al.* 2010; vanStaa 2011). On the other hand, parents might hold an inhibitory role, filtering information before it reaches the child, blocking the child's interaction by answering on the child's behalf, or reprimanding the child for butting in (Young *et al.* 2003; vanStaa 2011). Triadic communication presents great challenges for health professionals because it is often considered to be nothing more than multi-party talk where children are often passive bystanders (vanStaa 2011). Parents can also reside on the sideline of nurse–child interactions (Callery and Milnes 2012). Callery and Milnes (2012: 8) highlight the need to recognize the influence of dyadic relationships within triadic interactions between child, parent, and health professional:

> The dyads of nurse–parent, nurse–child and parent–child interact to form the triadic relationship that has features of a therapeutic alliance. There is potential for both cooperation and conflict in each of these dyadic relationships, with implications for the potential for alliances to be therapeutic.

Taking account of, and addressing, the needs of both child and parent(s) is central to the United Nations (1989) Convention on the Rights of the Child (UNCRC), which emphasizes the importance of listening to children and considering their views when planning services and making decisions, in addition to taking account of parents' responsibility to act in children's best interests.

Activity

During your clinical placement, observe an interaction between a parent, child, and another third party.

- Describe what happens. What do you see? Who talks to whom? What do you hear? Who says what?, etc.
- How does each person behave (verbally and non-verbally) when interacting with another (i.e. third party with parent, parent with child, third party with child)?

Communication messages

Verbal communications are messages imparted via language expressed as words. Words do not have the same meaning for everyone who hears them. Children often struggle to convey clearly what is important to them and you may not fully understand what they are trying to say. You may experience difficultly finding appropriate ways to discuss sensitive issues with children, leaving them unable to make sense of information presented (Lefevre 2010). Children less than 8 years of age interpret words concretely and frequently misinterpret medical terms (Mahan 1999). When communicating with families it is important to employ everyday, understandable language. Always check understanding of information exchanged with children and parents. It would be unhelpful to merely ask a child if they understand, since they are likely to answer 'yes' whether they understand or not. Some useful ways to validate understanding include:

- Ask the parent/child to repeat back to you what you have told them.
- Ask a series of open-ended questions to determine the parent's/child's knowledge.
- Use creative participatory methods (e.g. picture, word activity board, game) to determine the child's understanding.
- Observe the parent's/child's body language (e.g. movements, posture, eye contact, expressions).
- Involve the child's parents/guardians in interpreting the child's behaviour.
- Rephrase questions with words the parent/child uses.
- Paraphrase back to the parent/child what they said every so often to clarify meaning.
- Summarize the discussion at the end of long conversations.
- Ask the child what they would tell a friend if they had to explain it to them.

Non-verbal communications are messages imparted without resort to spoken language. Such communication encompasses body language (e.g. facial expressions, eye contact, body movements, and touch) and paralanguage (e.g. vocal tone, pitch, and pace). Non-verbal communication represents a large portion of any interaction, especially with children because children's communicative styles and skills are often less verbal and more demonstrative (Thomas 2001). Some children may struggle, or be unable, to convey their experiences and thoughts through words and may demonstrate these instead through gestures, facial expressions, and sounds (Lefevre 2010). It is important to approach children less than 2 years old slowly, using a calm, soothing voice to avoid startling them. Approach children aged 3–7 years at eye level to appear less threatening by de-emphasizing the child's small size. With older children (i.e. 8–12 years), avoid a facial expression that might convey disappointment or anger (Mahan 1999).

Interpersonal skills

The effective exchange of messages depends upon core interpersonal skills used by those involved, such as, questioning, explaining, reassuring, and listening.

Questioning

There are many different forms of questions that shift the interaction in diverse directions and yield distinctive responses. Closed questions are a directive type of exploration and are health professional driven and focused. They have a specific fact-finding purpose and can be quickly answered with short, monosyllabic responses, such as 'yes', 'no', 'not sure', or with a short phrase. While asking children and parents closed questions is legitimate to establish what is wrong with them and to instigate appropriate interventions, closed questions do not explore the child's and/or parent's agenda because their answer and involvement in the communication process is restricted (Faulkner 1998). This type of exploration can disempower the child and family.

Reflection point

Think about the answers you might get to the following closed questions and how these answers might affect your ability to engage with a child:

- Are you sore?
- Do you want something for pain?
- Have you eaten anything?
- Do you feel like eating anything?
- Did you have your operation?

Open-ended questions usually begin with 'what', 'why', 'could' or 'how', and request an answer of perception, information or feelings. Such questions invite children and families into the conversation at a more participative level. Open-ended questions bestow upon children and families the opportunity to talk freely about their experiences; things of interest or importance to them, as opposed to things of interest or importance to your agenda. Gathering parents' viewpoint is important because parents have knowledge and experience in detecting subtle changes in their child's behaviour and can make a valuable contribution to their child's care. Gathering children's views is of equal importance because children may have different objectives, preferences and, in some cases, may be in the best position to assert their own perspectives.

Reflection point

Think about the answers you might get to the following open questions and how these answers might influence your ability to engage with a child:

- Tell me about your pain.
- How you are feeling?
- What have you been eating?
- What do you feel like eating?
- How have you been since your operation?

Questioning also encompasses providing parents and children with an opportunity to ask questions. Children and their parents often have many questions about, for example, a forthcoming hospital admission, health clinic visit, operation or disease/condition (Fortier *et al.* 2009; Gordon *et al.* 2011). Sometimes children experience difficulties formulating questions and you might need to help them to do so (Beresford and Sloper 2003; Gibson *et al.* 2010).

Explaining

The provision of accurate and comprehensive information is an individual entitlement, and a prerequisite for children and parents increased participation in healthcare decisions that affect them directly (Mikkelsen and Frederiksen 2011). Although children and parents should have access to accurate and easily understandable information, the type and amount of information they want varies according to their different needs and individual desires for information (Lambert *et al.* 2008; Gordon *et al.* 2011).

Activity

Consider a boy or girl of middle to late childhood age you encountered during your clinical practice. Write a brief synopsis about how informed the child was of what was going on around them and/or their health condition and then answer the following questions:

- What, and how much, information was relayed to the child?
- Who relayed the information to the child?
- What format (e.g. verbal, written, drawings, creative methods) was used to relay information to the child?
- What words or tangible analogies (e.g. ligaments that move the knee joint are like an elastic band) were used to transmit the information?
- Where was the information relayed to the child?

Once you have written your brief synopsis consider whether things could have been done differently or better.

Some parents/children may actively seek out information, thus insufficient or a lack of information can lead to uncertainty and worry about what will happen. Other parents/children might resist information for fear of its potentially negative impact. The resistance of information might be considered a coping strategy, and excessive or inappropriate information could have negative consequences in increasing anxiety and insecurity. Sometimes, children and parents alike become overwhelmed with information received, especially on hearing bad news, at a time of illness diagnosis and/or poor prognosis (Hummelinck and Pollock 2006; Soanes *et al.* 2009). Children's and parents' worries and anxieties may impede their ability to absorb and/or remember information (Lowe *et al.* 2008). Thus, the provision of information needs to be sensitively individualized to parents' and children's needs, by addressing their information requirements but not increasing their anxiety or insecurity by relaying excessive information to them, or involving them in decision-making processes beyond their desire. It is important to assess individual child and family information preferences, present information in small pieces frequently, repeat as needed, and continue to build on and scaffold information for families.

Parents have an important role as information provider for their child, often acting as an intermediary between their child and health professional, transmitting and translating information. You must not assume that parents are always confident and/or competent undertaking this information provider role (Tourigny *et al.* 2005; Gordon *et al.* 2011). Parents need to be adequately supported, prepared, and informed so that they can accurately answer their child's questions and meet their child's informational needs.

Reassuring

Health professionals frequently tell children and parents that what they are doing will make them or their children better. While children and parents value such reassurance, you need to be aware of the difference between optimistic/reflexive and false/premature reassurance. While optimistic/reflexive reassurance focuses on protecting the patient, false reassurance centres on protecting the health professional (Teasdale 1989; Morse *et al.* 1992; Fareed 1996). False or premature reassurance can result in the marginalization of children and families by failing to address issues of concern to them. This dismisses, belittles, and minimizes any worries/feelings families may have. There is the risk that if children come to believe that expressing and sharing their views and concerns are not permissible, they will carry this conception forward into their adult life (Petrie 2011). By offering parents and children an opportunity to express their views and feelings, it is possible to demonstrate to them that those views and feelings are legitimate. Not offering children an opportunity to voice their concerns and worries means children and families often feel not listened to.

Activity

Consider the following short interaction between a nurse and John aged 10 and answer the questions that follow.

Nurse: How are you? Are you okay?
Child: I might have to get my appendix out [holding tummy].
Nurse: Oh, you look like a strong boy.

- What do you think about the nurse's approach in this interaction?
- Was John offered an opportunity to voice his concerns?
- Is there anything you think John might have been worried about?
- How would you have responded to John?

Did your analysis match the following?

The nurse neglected to explore John's concerns, worries or feeling about having his impending operation. John is extremely anxious and scared about what will happen. He now conceals his worries and feelings about his impending surgery because he wants to be brave and strong. The nurse could have picked up on John's 'cue' to open a conversation with him about having to have an operation; for instance, 'You might have to have your appendix taken out, how do you feel about that?'

Listening

Children have a right to be heard and have their views taken into account in decisions that affect them, and parents have responsibilities, rights, and duties to provide appropriate direction and guidance and act in the best interests of their children (Lundy 2007). Yet there is evidence within healthcare provision that children's right to be listened to is not always embraced (Kilkelly and Donnelly 2006). One of the most important elements of listening to children and including them in decisions is *respect*. To ensure children are engaged in dialogue, Thomas (2001) recommends that you should:

- accept that all children have the *right* to be included;
- look actively for children's *competence* rather than assume incompetence;
- use *methods of communication* that children find helpful/enjoyable;
- give children *time* to express their views in their own way; and
- treat children, and their views, with *respect*.

If you don't have sufficient time to listen to a child you should, explain this to them and suggest an alternative time when you will be able to offer them your undivided attention. When children are allowed time to express their views, are listened to, and offered realistic choices, their felt need to protest is minimized (Mahan 1999). To actively listen to children, value silences to allow them time to think about what they want to say, avoid interrupting them by waiting for natural pauses in conversation to intervene, do not interrupt to hurry them along or attempt to finish their sentences for them, and observe their body language, movements, gestures, and facial expressions.

Reflection point

Reflect for five minutes on why it is important to listen to children.

A child-centred approach to communication

When communicating with children and families, you must ensure your approach is appropriate to each child's age and developmental needs. Give attention to the vocabulary you use. Use short, clear sentences and everyday language as opposed to long, complex medical descriptions, which can be confusing to children. Take care when communicating with young people to ensure your approach is not too baby-like. Young people often find this patronizing, as if you are speaking down to them. Some children, especially when they are older, are more confident, articulate, and speak more freely than others, who are shyer, less articulate, and tend to respond with shorter and less in-depth answers. Sometimes children might appear reluctant to talk, answer monosyllabically or with 'I don't know'. Although there are many reasons why children become non-communicative (e.g. unfamiliarity with health professional, lack of interest in the topic of discussion), one factor is the unequal power divide that exists between children and adults. The relative powerlessness of children makes them suspicious of adult questions and susceptible to saying what they think adults want to hear (Thomas 2001). Non-communication, withholding of information, and sidestepping adults' agendas are strategies children use to enhance their power base (McLeod 2008).

Activity

Select a procedure (e.g. recording of vital signs, lumbar puncture, wound dress-ing). Devise a plan about how you are going to prepare a 7-year-old child for this procedure. For instance, think of the words you might use to inform a 7-year-old about your selected procedure. Besides verbal communication, con-sider practical ways to demonstrate the procedure to the child, including ways to actively involve the child in this demonstration.

Creative participatory tools offer valuable additions to any engagements with children (Beddoes *et al.* 2010; Winter 2011). This might involve the incorporation of visual aids, play, arts and crafts, drawings, and/or various technologies. Engaging with children through such participatory media is a valuable means of getting to know them, building rapport and trust. Children are naturally cautious of strangers and will be reluctant to disclose information when they are suspicious of, afraid of or do not know adults. Rapport is a two-way process. From the beginning, ensure the child knows who you are, what your job is, and the purpose of your visit to them (Winter 2011). Children appreciate it when health professionals make an effort to learn about them as people and not just as patients (Gibson *et al.* 2010). Building rapport is a crucial part of forming trusting relationships with children (McLeod 2008), and means creating a connection that facilitates confidence and cooperation between parties engaged in verbal and non-verbal communication (Winter 2011).

Table 1.1 LEARN mnemonic

- **Listen** with sympathy and understanding to the family's perception of the problem
- **Explain** appropriate information about the care strategy to the family
- **Acknowledge** family explanations and discuss similarities with and differences to health professionals' explanations
- **Recommend through negotiation** a treatment plan that takes account of both patient and health professional explanations

Source: Adapted from Ahmann (1994)

Activity

- Why is it important to build rapport with children?
- How might you earn a child's respect and build trust?
- What barriers might you encounter in developing rapport with children?
- How might you overcome some of these barriers?

Models of communication for use in child health contexts

Two models adapted by Ahmann (1994) for use within the context of family centred care to assist with building collaborative communication with parents are LEARN (Table 1.1) and the Nursing Mutual Participation Model of Care (Table 1.2).

Activity

During your current or next clinical placement, follow Steps 1–4 of the Nursing Mutual Participation Model of Care to communicate with a parent about their child's care. Record brief notes on the parent's response and note your thoughts and ideas to discuss with your clinical preceptor/mentor/supervisor.

Table 1.2 Nursing Mutual Participation Model of Care

Step 1: Use open-ended questions to establish a caring atmosphere
- How is it going for you?

Step 2: Use direct questions to ascertain parental goals and expectations
- How did you hope I could help you [parent/your child] today?

Step 3: Assess parent's perception of child's illness through questions
- How does your child look to you today?
- How do you think your child is doing?

Step 4: Elicit parent's suggestions/preferences and invite participation in care
- Do you have any suggestions concerning your child's care?
- Is there anything you personally wish to do for or with your child?

Source: Adapted from Ahmann (1994)

Table 1.3 Nursing Approaches: Involvement in Care

- **Communicating/nurse-centred – *permission*:** nurses are authoritative and controlling – they assess parents' wishes but only allow parent involvement on their terms
- **Non-communicating/nurse-centred – *exclusion*:** nurses exclude parents
- **Non-communicating/person-centred – *assumption*:** nurses make subjective assumptions of family needs with no record of systematic assessment
- **Communicating/person-centred – *negotiation*:** nurses communicate and share expertise/knowledge and listen to families

Source: Adapted from Casey (1995)

Casey's (1995) Nursing Approaches model illustrates the effect that communication and nursing style can have on parents' involvement in their child's care (Table 1.3).

Reflection point

Think about Casey's nursing approaches. It might be helpful to read Casey's paper to help with your reflection. Identify examples from your clinical placements to support or refute Casey's four levels of parental involvement.

- Permission
- Exclusion
- Assumption
- Negotiation

Based on your examples, reflect on the advantages and disadvantages of adapting each of Casey's nursing approaches when communicating with parents.

The Parent–Staff Model of Paediatric Care, developed by Alsop-Shields (2002), is a way of viewing the family and interacting with them rather than a way of delivering any specific type of care. There are two main components to the model – parents' presence and communication between staff and parents. The core element of the model is the view of the parent and child as a single, unified entity. They are in hospital [the environment] surrounded by hospital staff – a separate entity/unit. Communication is the linking factor between these two entities – that is, parent–child entity and staff unit. Health (or depletion of it) is inherent within the model. Within this model, the action is the communication between parents and staff.

In an attempt to improve partnerships with children and families, Figueroa-Altman *et al.* (2005) devised the mnemonic KIDSCARE to represent actions nurses could take to promote relationships with children and their families (Table 1.4).

Table 1.4 KIDSCARE mnemonic

- **Knock** before entering a family's temporary personal territory
- **Introduce** yourself by name, role, length of shift
- **Determine** how patient/family like to be addressed
- **Safety** – demonstrate strict adherence to safety standards and explain reasons for them
- **Clean** hands in front of patient/family
- **Advocate** for family concerns, use open questions to elicit family preferences
- **Respond** – let families know your availability and accessibility
- **Explain** what you are going to do, allow time for questions, involve family

Source: Adapted from Figueroa-Altman *et al.* (2005)

Activity

During your current or next clinical placement, follow Figueroa-Altman and colleagues' mnemonic KIDSCARE to initiate an encounter with a child and their family. Write a brief synopsis of your experience to discuss with your clinical preceptor/mentor/supervisor.

While many models focus on collaborative interactions with parents, following conversations with several children (aged 4–17 years) about communicating with healthcare professionals, Sydnor-Greenberg and Dokken (2001) proposed the CLEAR model of communication, which illustrates what children would prefer in their interactions with health professionals (Table 1.5).

Activity

Consider the first concept of Sydnor-Greenberg and Dokken's CLEAR model – *Context.* How might you develop your ability to engage with a child about their life? What would you discuss socially with the child?

To help answer these questions, use various resources (e.g. TV guides, bookstores, toy stores, websites, etc.) to identify what is current in the child's world (e.g. toys, characters, TV programmes, children's books, technologies, games, sports). Don't just identify what's in vogue, experience it! Read a children's book. Watch a children's programme. Play a child's electronic game. Follow up on this activity by having a conversation with a child.

- Was your search accurate?
- Did you find out what it was that attracted the child to his or her interests?
- Did knowing something about the child's world help you in engaging socially with them?

Table 1.5 CLEAR model

- **Context** – regard the child as a whole person by asking questions about their life (i.e. school, friends, and activities) outside the illness they are experiencing
- **Listening** – listen to and include children
- **Empowerment** – communicate directly with children and provide them with information to prepare them for what is to happen, what you are going to do, and what they themselves will be able to do
- **Advice and Reassurance** – offer health promotion advice and reassure children about their health

Source: Adapted from Sydnor-Greenberg and Dokken (2001)

Investigating 6- to 16-year-olds' experiences of communicating with health professionals in hospital, Lambert *et al.* (2011) devised the Child Transitional Communication (CTC) model, which is underpinned by two components: (1) a *visible-ness* construct and (2) five theoretical bodies of knowledge (Figure 1.1) .

1. *Visible-ness* represents the extent of children's inclusion or exclusion in the communication process, in addition to the degree to which children's

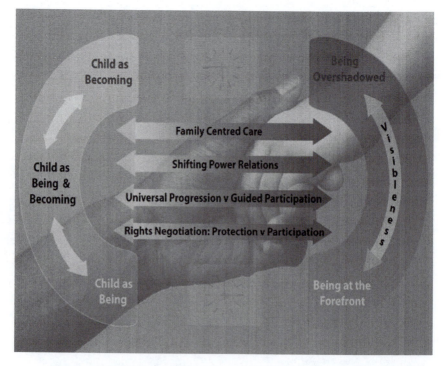

Figure 1.1 Child Transitional Communication (CTC) model (Lambert 2009)

communication needs are met (Lambert *et al.* 2008). Children can occupy one of two positions in the communication process:

- a background overshadowed position in which children are marginal to the communication process as *passive bystanders*; or
- a forefront position in which children are *active participants* in the communication process.

2. In an attempt to explain why children might occupy either a passive bystander or an active participant position in the communication process, Lambert *et al.* (2011) identified conflicting dichotomies within *five theoretical bodies of knowledge*:

- *Family centred care*: child as family member vs. child as unique entity.
- *Shifting power relations:* child as powerless vs. empowered child.
- *Universal progression versus guided participation:* child as immature, incompetent, and dependent vs. child as mature, competent, and independent.
- *Rights negotiation – protection versus participation:* child as having a right to protection vs. child as having a right to liberation.
- *Child as being and/or becoming:* child as becoming vs. child as being.

Reflection point

In considering the child as *becoming* vs. *being,* reflect on the following:

- What is your stance on children in society today?
- How do you think children are portrayed in society?
- What are your thoughts on communicating with children?
- Is there any overlap between how you think children are portrayed in society and your thoughts about communicating with children?

Uprichard (2008) questions the dichotomy of child as becoming vs. child as being and argues that the conflicting discourses of child as being vs. child as becoming should be considered together, each complementing the other. Uprichard (2008: 303) argues that 'understanding the "child" as both "being and becoming" increases the agency that child has in the world'.

Read Uprichard's paper and reflect on the following

- How might you integrate the two perspectives of child as being and child as becoming when communicating with children and their families?
- How can understanding the child as both being and becoming increase the agency that children might have in the communication process?
- Why is it important to build and value children's agency?

Lambert *et al.* (2011) argue that these conflicting dichotomies are reflective of an overarching tension between the two discourses *protection* and *participation*. For instance, viewing children as *being* and/or *becoming* reflects tensions between the need to protect and safeguard (i.e. becoming), while simultaneously respecting the child's right to participate (i.e. being). This presents an extreme challenge because in developing partnerships with children and families, you must not only acknowledge the participatory rights of children but also work to protect children from distress/upset and recognize the responsibility and rights of parents as children's principal guardians. This is important because children frequently move between being – or wanting to be – a *passive bystander* or an *active participant* in the communication process depending on the situation they find themselves in (Lambert *et al.* 2008).

Applied within the context of educational decision-making, Lundy's (2007) model provides an effective way for conceptualizing Article 12 of the UNCRC by considering other relevant provisions [i.e. Article 2 (non-discrimination), Article 13 (right to information), Article 3 (best interests), Article 5 (right to guidance) and Article 19 (right to be safe)] alongside four key factors: space, voice, audience, and influence.

- *Space*: Children must be given the opportunity to express a view.
- *Voice*: Children must be facilitated to express their views.
- *Audience*: The view must be listened to.
- *Influence*: The view must be acted upon, as appropriate.

Gibson *et al.* (2010) presented a supplementary model to highlight the evolution of communication roles in children's and young people's cancer care.

- Young children (age 4–5 years) rely on parents to communicate with health professionals.
- Older children (age 6–12 years) wish to communicate directly with health professionals, yet parents often assume the lead role.
- Young people (age 13–19 years) take the lead role in communicating with health professionals over their parents.

Gibson *et al.* contended that children remain in the background until they become young people and begin to gain independence, responsibility, and autonomy. As young people mature, they want a more visible foreground role and take on many communicative roles themselves (Figure 1.2).

Gibson and colleagues' (2010: 1405) age groupings are 'not fixed as it is recognised not all children are the same. Progression may therefore occur earlier or later than the ages specified'. This is important because age does not always reflect the extent to which children want to be included in the communication process (Lambert *et al.* 2008). The optimal role for children to assume is transitory, contextual, and based on each child's individual preferences and needs at any given time (Lambert *et al.* 2011). You will need to be flexible in your interactions with children and establish each child's individual preferences by continually engaging in a reciprocal process of assessment and reassessment. This will assist with capturing

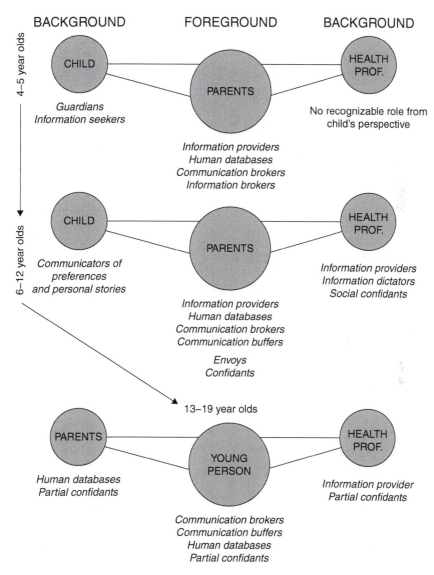

Figure 1.2 Communication roles in children's and young people's cancer care (reprinted with permission from Gibson *et al.* 2010; © 2010 Elsevier)

the extent the child wishes to be involved – or not – in the communication process and their ongoing needs. Assessment will assist with interpreting Article 12 in conjunction with Article 5 of the UNCRC – ensuring that children are provided with appropriate adult direction and guidance consistent with their evolving capacities (Lundy 2007).

Activity

Think about how, what, and when you would assess children's communication needs and their individual preferences for involvement and information. What would you document about your assessment, where and how?

Did you consider verbal interactions and questioning, creative participatory methods, non-verbal cues, parent involvement, and/or how the child normally communicates?

Conclusion

Effective communication is crucial for the delivery of quality nursing care and the establishment of child–parent–health professional partnerships. This chapter has highlighted some of the core elements of communication and interpersonal skills, alongside key theoretical perspectives and models of communication, to consider when engaging with children and their families.

Key messages

- Children's right to consultation and participation needs to be recognized in conjunction with children's right to protection and parents' rights and responsibility as principal guardians.
- Attention must be given to children's developmental, cognitive, and linguistic abilities and the various mediums of communication available to facilitate interaction according to each child's preferred mode of communication.
- Individual children and family preferences need to be assessed continuously to identify changing communication needs at different points in time.

References

Ahmann, E. (1994) Family-centered care: shifting orientation, *Pediatric Nursing*, 20(2): 113–17.

Alsop-Shields, L. (2002) The parent–staff interaction model of paediatric care, *Journal of Pediatric Nursing*, 17(6): 442–9.

Beddoes, D., Hedges, A., Sloman, J., Smith, L. and Smith, T. (2010) *Engaging Children and Young People in Research and Consultation: A Review of Principles, Policy and Practice*. OPM #7866. London: General Teaching Council for England.

Beresford, B.A. and Sloper, P. (2003) Chronically ill adolescents' experiences of communicating with doctors: a qualitative study, *Journal of Adolescent Health*, 33(3): 172–9.

Callery, P. and Milnes, L. (2012) Communication between nurses, children and their parents in asthma review consultations, *Journal of Clinical Nursing*, 21(11/12): 1641–50.

Casey, A. (1995) Partnership nursing; influences on involvement of informal carers, *Journal of Advanced Nursing*, 22(6): 1058–62.

Fareed, A. (1996) The experience of reassurance: patients' perspectives, *Journal of Advanced Nursing*, 23(2): 272–9.

Faulkner, A. (1998) *Effective Interaction with Patients*, 2nd edn. Edinburgh: Churchill Livingstone.

Figueroa-Altman, A.R., Bedrossian, L., Steinmiller, E.A. and Wilmot, S.M. (2005) KIDS CARE: improving partnerships with children and families, *American Journal of Nursing*, 105(6): 72A–72C.

Fortier, M., MacLaren Chorney, J., Zisk Rony, R., Perret-Karimi, D., Rinehart, J., Camilon, F.S. *et al.* (2009) Children's desire for perioperative information, *Anesthesia and Analgesia*, 109(4): 1085–90.

Gabe, J., Olumide, G. and Bury, M. (2004) ' It takes three to tango': a framework for understanding patient partnership in paediatric clinics, *Social Science and Medicine*, 59(5): 1071–9.

Gibson, F., Aldiss, S., Horstman, M., Kumpunen, S. and Richardson, A. (2010) Children and young people's experiences of cancer care: a qualitative research study using participatory methods, *International Journal of Nursing Studies*, 47: 1397–407.

Gordon, B.K., Jaaniste, T., Bartlett, K., Perrin, M., Jackson, A., Sandstrom, A. *et al.* (2011) Child and parental surveys about pre-hospitalisation information provision, *Child: Care, Health and Development*, 37(5): 727–33.

Hemphill, A.L. and Dearmun, A.K. (2006) Working with children and their families, in A. Glasper and J. Richardson (eds) *A Textbook of Children's and Young People's Nursing*. London: Churchill Livingstone/Elsevier.

Hummelinck, A. and Pollock, K. (2006) Parents' information needs about the treatment of their chronically ill child: a qualitative study, *Patient Education and Counselling*, 62(2): 228–34.

Kilkelly, U. and Donnelly, M. (2006) *The Child's Right to be Heard in the Healthcare Setting: Perspectives of Children, Parents and Health Professionals*. Dublin: Office of the Minister for Children.

Lambert, V. (2009) *'Visible-ness': The Nature of Communication between Children and Health Professionals in a Specialist Children's Hospital in the Republic of Ireland: An Ethnographic Inquiry*, PhD thesis, Trinity College Dublin.

Lambert, V., Glacken, M. and McCarron, M. (2008) ' Visible-ness': the nature of communication for children admitted to a specialist paediatric hospital in the Republic of Ireland, *Journal of Clinical Nursing*, 17(23): 3092–102.

Lambert, V., Glacken, M. and McCarron, M. (2011) Communication between children and health professionals in a child hospital setting: a Child Transitional Communication (CTC) model, *Journal of Advanced Nursing*, 67(3): 569–82.

Lefevre, M. (2010) *Communicating with Children and Young People: Making a Difference*. Bristol: Policy Press.

Lowe, R., Bravery, K. and Gibson, F. (2008) Navigating the maze: parents' views and influence on a paediatric haematology and oncology day care service, *Journal of Clinical Nursing*, 17: 3159–67.

Lundy, L. (2007) ' Voice' is not enough: conceptualising Article 12 of the United Nations Convention on the Rights of the Child, *British Educational Research Journal*, 33(6): 927–42.

Mahan, C.C. (1999) Communication, in M.E. Broome and J.A. Rollins (eds) *Core Curriculum for the Nursing Care of Children and Their Families*. Pitman, NJ: Jannetti Publications.

McLeod, A. (2008) *Listening to Children: A Practitioner's Guide*. London: Jessica Kingsley.

Mikkelsen, G. and Frederiksen, K. (2011) Family-centred care of children in hospital – a concept analysis, *Journal of Advanced Nursing*, 67(5): 1152–62.

Morse, J.M., Bottorff, J., Anderson, G., O'Brien, B. and Solberg, S. (1992) Beyond empathy: expanding expressions of caring, *Journal of Advanced Nursing*, 17(7): 809–21.

Petrie, P. (2011) *Communication Skills for Working with Children and Young People*. London: Jessica Kingsley.

Pyorala, E. (2004) The participation roles of children and adolescents in the dietary counselling of diabetics, *Patient Education and Counselling*, 55(3): 385–95.

Shelton, T.L., Jeppson, E.S. and Johnson, B.H. (1987) *Family-Centred Care for Children with Special Health Care Needs*. Washington, DC: Association for the Care of Children's Health and Institution for Family Centered Care (IFCC) in the USA.

Soanes, L., Hargrave, D., Smith, L. and Gibson, F. (2009) What are the experiences of the child with a brain tumour and their parents?, *European Journal of Oncology Nursing*, 13: 255–61.

Sydnor-Greenberg, N. and Dokken, D.L. (2001) Communication in healthcare: thoughts on the child's perspective, *Journal of Child and Family Nursing*, 4(2): 225–30.

Teasdale, K. (1989) The concept of reassurance in nursing, *Journal of Advanced Nursing*, 14(6): 444–50.

Thomas, N. (2001) Listening to children, in P. Foley, J. Roche and S. Tucker (eds) *Children in Society: Contemporary Theory, Policy and Practice*. Basingstoke: Palgrave/Open University Press.

Tourigny, J., Chapados, C. and Pineault, R. (2005) Determinants of parental behaviour when children undergo day-care surgery, *Journal of Advanced Nursing*, 52(5): 490–7.

United Nations (1989) *United Nations Convention on the Rights of the Child*. Geneva: United Nations.

Uprichard, E. (2008) Children as 'being and becomings': children, childhood and temporality, *Children and Society*, 22(4): 303–13.

vanStaa, A. (2011) Unravelling triadic communication in hospital consultations with adolescents with chronic conditions: the added value of mixed methods research, *Patient Education and Counselling*, 82: 455–64.

Winter, K. (2011) *Building Relationships and Communicating with Young Children: A Practical Guide for Social Workers*. London: Routledge.

Young, B., Dixon-Woods, M., Windridge, K.C. and Heney, D. (2003) Managing communication with young people who have a potentially life threatening chronic illness: qualitative study of patients and parents, *British Medical Journal*, 326(7384): 305–8.

2 Communicating with children in early and middle childhood

Noírín Hayes and Philomena Keogh

This chapter starts from the belief that communication is a core nursing skill and one that requires particular attention when infants and young children are involved. For the purposes of this chapter, childhood is defined as the period from birth through to 8–10 years and, where appropriate, we present information specific to infants, toddlers, preschoolers and young children. The importance of self-awareness, the special case of culture, and the role of play in communicating with children are considered. We explore communication with children from a developmental perspective and suggest activities, strategies, and approaches to improve and enhance communication skills.

Learning outcomes

By the end of this chapter you should be able to:

1. Describe children's development in relation to their ability to communicate
2. Develop greater self-awareness in your communication with babies and young children
3. Practise and value the use of play when working with young children
4. Be aware of cultural differences when working with families

---

Introduction

When working with babies and young children, good communication is crucial to their overall development. This involves developing and maintaining relationships, conducting accurate assessments, providing advice and information in a developmentally appropriate manner, and creating opportunities for the expression of feelings and preferences. These opportunities are only effective and therapeutic if the process of communication is understood, and the professional has excellent self-awareness and appropriate interpersonal skills. Working with children requires active engagement with their families to help them cope with the reality of illness and its consequences. Corlett and Twycross (2006) highlight that although parents want to be involved in their children's care, often nurses' lack of communication and limited negotiation means that this does not always happen. Family centred care is a basic principle of contemporary children's nursing and health care. It recognizes that nursing care is most effective if done in conjunction with the child's family. It is a partnership approach that is founded on good communication between healthcare staff and the family. While nurses and parents believe in the ethos of family centred care, differences often exist between how parents and nurses view their roles (Hughes 2007). Effective communication can help clarify roles and resolve ambiguity. Nurses must be sensitive to the concerns and anxieties that parents have but which they might not always be able to express or articulate. A deep self-understanding is necessary before it is possible to develop an understanding of others (i.e. children, families, colleagues).

Self-awareness

'Knowing others is wisdom, knowing thyself is enlightenment'. This ancient Chinese phrase, which is attributed to the philosopher Lao Tzu (600 B.C.), emphasizes the importance and value of self-awareness. Self-awareness involves both a personal development skill, with the focus on increasing awareness of yourself, and a developmental process of understanding your own beliefs, values, and motivations, while developing an understanding of how these affect others. McPherson (2010: 16) stresses that 'to provide child centred healthcare, professionals must have an awareness of their own behaviour and interactions with children and their families'. Self-awareness can be conceptualized both as a personality trait and a skill involving a dynamic relationship between what kind of person you think you are, how you feel about yourself, and the verbal and non-verbal behaviour you use and connect with. Ricks and Charlesworth (2003: 23) discuss an emergent self – a changing self that is influenced by experiences and purposeful awareness. Learning about yourself and the intentional use of self in your professional role can be enhanced in a number of ways, including:

- being a reflective practitioner and engaging in reflexivity more generally;
- using reflection as a process of self-awareness and consciousness (you could keep a reflective diary);
- closely observing what others do;
- actively listening to what others are saying (paying attention to non-verbal body language);
- giving and receiving feedback in a personal and professional manner. This can be helpful in relation to your self-conception and can help distinguish what you are versus what you think you are.

Some possible barriers to self-awareness include:

- allowing your beliefs, values, and attitudes to get in the way of communicating clearly;

- adopting a defensive mode and thereby not hearing what the parent or child is saying to you; this can block constructive criticism from which you could learn and improve self-awareness;
- thinking that you fully understand the situation of the parent or the child without asking them.

Reflection point

Use the following questions to help you understand and explore your own values and attitudes (OMCYA 2006):

Can I:

- be comfortable sharing feelings and experiences about bias or discrimination?
- stand back, examine and objectively discuss my own ethnicity and culture?
- stand up for myself if I am a target of discrimination?
- identify unfair and untrue images, comments, and behaviours made about people from minority backgrounds?
- identify and empathize with adults and children affected by discrimination and racism?
- recognize that there are unequal power relations within society?
- explain what prejudice, racism, and discrimination mean?
- identify acceptable and unacceptable behaviours in a professional context (e.g. discussion in relation to the child or family)?
- recognize excuses or objections to avoid doing this work within myself and from others around me?

Recognizing your own basic needs, sensitivity to context, and self-awareness is central to understanding others and creating and developing a common ground of experience. Coyne (2006) noted that parents found that the demeanour of nurses altered as their child's condition changed. These changes in demeanour, or body language, convey powerful messages and are especially important in, for example, the case of inter-cultural communication where shared verbal language may be limited.

Awareness of cultural differences

Cultural differences between nursing and patient populations in need of culturally relevant care cannot be ignored. Embracing diversity and ensuring equality in healthcare settings is essential. Acknowledging, accepting, and responding appropriately to difference have enormous implications for children and their families in a healthcare environment. Practitioners are important role models and

children will actively learn from them how to behave and communicate respectfully towards others (OMCYA 2006).

Language is one of the most important differences between cultures, and one of
the greatest barriers. Linguistic conventions may cause significant misunderstand-
ings related, for example, to speech acts, interaction management, vocabulary used,
and forms of politeness. To be a respectful inter-cultural communicator, it is important not only for you to be aware of how your own cultural perspectives influence
your awareness of other cultures, but also to be open to new and different communication experiences. It is necessary to be able to adapt your habits and behaviour
to engage successfully with children and parents from different cultures. There are
differences in the amount of directness/indirectness we choose when communicating and differences in how we view and behave towards health, illness, and
death. For example, the usual question-and-answer approach adopted when determining, for instance, a medical history in the West, is not used in all cultures.
Nurses must look at ways in which they view difference and reflect on their own
thoughts regarding diversity and equality. Health professionals can create inclusive
and welcoming environments for children and their parents that support equality
and difference by considering the following:

- building up a library of books and tapes in a variety of languages;
- playing music from different cultures on the unit and inviting children and
  parents to contribute CDs;
- providing musical instruments from different countries;
- keeping art materials to hand for children to use and talk about their images,
  using a range of skin tones in pencils, crayons, and markers;
- displaying photographs of children and their families at a suitable level to
  prompt discussion with children.

Respecting children's rights, needs, and development

Communication occurs both informally and formally in healthcare settings, with
adults frequently communicating in a neutral and objective manner while gathering or imparting facts as they seek to find solutions. Children, on the other hand,
are more likely to communicate while engaged and busy with another activity; they
use fewer words and rely on non-verbal as well as verbal communication. Children
respond better to effective communication that is warm, caring, engaging, and
trusting. Communicating with children about their illness is important because this
can provide particular insights into their condition that may be missed by relying
on parental reports (Riley 2004). Children have a right to be involved in decisions
taken that affect them (United Nations 1989). This means 'informing children,
listening to them and actively involving children who have views in making decisions about their care' (Alderson 1993: 3). Enable children to be part of discussions
about their treatments so that they feel part of the process. They will use whatever
information is given to them to try to make sense of their situation, and an inability to completely understand does not justify a lack of discussion with a child who
wishes to be involved. This can even be done with very young children as you talk

them through the processes, even when they do not – or cannot – respond. At all times use clear, simple, and unemotional language in a confident and unhurried way and try to avoid medical jargon. Remember that there are no wrong questions from children, and if they ask questions they probably sense something is not right and may be exploring who they can trust. Seemingly minor questions about, for example, post-operative appearance or types of bandage to be used can, in fact, be very important to the child and should be respected and answered clearly and carefully.

Play as a means of communication

Play is a central activity in the lives of all young children. It is a context for communication, understanding, and catharsis and one that you should not underestimate. Become comfortable with the use of play as a form of communication and learn to facilitate children's play by using different toys and aids to develop a trusting relationship. Playing is the universal language for children and therefore it is important that nurses make time and feel comfortable initiating and supporting children's play. Play is a process through which children make sense of their world, practise for the future, and communicate feelings they may not be able to verbalize. For successful and effective communication with children, it is necessary to establish a good relationship with them, even when their encounter with the healthcare setting is short. This can be done by adopting an informal, chatty style both with the children and their parents (Fenwick *et al.* 2001) and engaging in a variety of activities such as playing games, drawing, and reading stories (Coyne *et al.* 2009). Observing children at play can often provide insight into how they are thinking and how they understand and cope with experiences and new situations. When a child is ill, play has a particularly important role in helping them understand and cope with what is happening, as well as during recovery. At a very basic level, play can act as a distraction for children, but it can also have a more direct role in helping children prepare for different medical procedures and in the recovery process.

Play is particularly useful in helping young children to become familiar with medical routines (IAHPS/CHI 2000). It can reduce stress, facilitate communication, and act as a useful source of information for the observant adult. For instance, X-ray procedures may be frightening for children. Play with dolls, books, and some equipment in advance of a medical procedure can help moderate the fear of the unknown. Carefully planned play opportunities allow children to express their feelings and promote positive coping strategies. Most play can be adapted to accommodate the needs of different children but it takes time and planning and a real regard for the value of play. Babies who are long-stay in healthcare settings, nursed in isolation or in intensive care are in need of particular support, and benefit from playful interactions appropriate to their particular condition.

In providing realistic and useful play opportunities for children, it is necessary to recognize that play takes time. Play that has a therapeutic value for children in helping them assimilate what is fearful and unknown needs to be carefully planned. Play specialists can provide advice on how best to create interesting play opportunities for children and develop exciting play and learning environments. It is helpful for play specialists and nurses to work together in planning for the play needs of young children and ensuring that the opportunities provided by play contexts can be used to maximize the effectiveness of communication around medical issues. Play specialists can also assist children in finding appropriate play activities and techniques to help make a healthcare experience a positive one. Advice on play strategies can be obtained from the various play associations (e.g. Children in Hospital Ireland, Action for Sick Children in the UK) and other websites on play (e.g. International Play Association England, Wales and Northern Ireland, Play England, and Sugradh in Ireland). In cooperation with play specialists and volunteers, nursing staff can improve the healthcare experience for children and their families through thoughtful and respectful use of communication and the appropriate use of play as a means of communication.

Activity

During your current, or future, clinical placement in a child healthcare setting:

- Carry out an audit of the play facilities and equipment.
- Profile the children and the use of play.
- Discuss with your preceptor/mentor/clinical supervisor the appropriateness of the materials available as a mechanism for enhanced communication.
- Highlight any examples of good practice noticed while carrying out the audit.

Developmental approaches to communication

Nurses need to understand child development and use this knowledge to maximize their interactions with children. Communication techniques vary depending on the age and developmental stage a child has reached (Table 2.1).

Communicating with infants

Respond to crying in a timely fashion

In infancy, a timely response to crying is necessary to develop good communication skills. Crying is a powerful signal pre-verbal infants use to communicate and get an immediate response. Infants cry in an attempt to gain some control over their environment, and if they are left to cry they miss an important opportunity for learning (Petrie 2011). You must give consideration to different cultural norms for interpreting and responding to crying and become aware of how parents manage this behaviour (Zeskind 1983). Having an understanding of the reasons infants cry (e.g. hunger, tiredness, boredom, pain, discomfort) is crucial to how you will respond. Other means infants will use to engage you include:

- vocalizing other sounds (e.g. cooing);
- making and holding eye contact;

Table 2.1 Communication techniques for children at different developmental stages

Age	Communication technique
Infants	Respond to crying in a timely fashion Allow infants time to warm up to you Use play and playful persuasion Use a soothing and calming tone when speaking to an infant Talk to the baby directly
Toddlers	Approach toddlers carefully, as they are often fearful and quite resistant Use the toddler's particular words for objects or actions so that they are better able to understand Use storytelling, dolls, and books Prepare toddlers for procedures just before they are about to occur
Preschoolers	Use play, puppetry, and storytelling for the third-party approach to engaging with children at this age Speak honestly Use simple, connected terms Allow the child to have choices, as appropriate Prepare preschoolers about one hour before procedures
School-age	Use diagrams, illustrations, and books Allow child to express feelings Use third-party stories to elicit desired information Allow child to ask questions related to care and treatment and allow adequate time for answering Prepare child a few days in advance of procedures

Source: Adapted from Scott-Ricci and Kyle (2008)

- using facial expressions including grimacing;
- blowing raspberries;
- moving their body;
- making gestures.

Through observation and listening, you will develop a deep understanding of infants' behaviour patterns and cues and develop an awareness of infants' sensitivity and tolerance for stimulation, such as touch, smell, taste, movement, and visual stimuli.

Allow infants time to warm up to you

To create a communication-rich environment, nurses must spend time getting to know infants and gaining their confidence. Be present while parents are with their infant as often as possible and encourage parents to include you in interactions with their infant. This will help the infant relax and trust you as a caring adult (Levetown 2008). You can also use this time to observe and register how parents manage communication with their infant. Parents can provide valuable personal information on specific interests and fears their infant may have and on personal language used to describe activities, body parts, and body functions. Using these familiar words can facilitate communication, particularly with a shy or quiet infant. Be alert to cultural differences and nuances used by parents. Ask parents about the preferences of their infant regarding regular routines. For example, do they hold the infant's hand while the infant is going to sleep, or sing a song or read a bedtime story? Should the light be left on or switched off? Has their infant a preference for music on a cot mobile? Does their infant have a favourite toy or blanket? When you are talking to parents, remember to include their infant in the conversation. On your own, when you approach an infant always establish and maintain eye contact and speak directly to them using infant-directed speech (a higher pitch, short phrases, simple words, and long vowels) before you make any physical contact with them. Do leave pauses for infants to respond.

Use play and playful persuasion

The human face never ceases to amaze infants and from a very early age they concentrate on the facial expressions of their adult carer. A face with a broad smile is always acceptable to infants and using other facial expressions to show wonderment/surprise (wide eyes) or delight by clapping or singing positively supports the communication process. Infants love the sound of the human voice, so chat away to them whenever you are close enough for them to hear.

Activity

Try out the following non-verbal interaction.

Hold an infant about 20–30 centimetres from your face. Wait until you have their full attention and then stick your tongue out. Infants as young as a few weeks old respond by copying you and sticking their tongue out too.

At about 4–5 months infants begin to use signals to indicate their needs and wants, such as raising their arms when they want to be picked up, or kicking their chair when they tire sitting in it. They will use body language such as turning away or breaking eye contact to indicate they have had enough playtime, stimulation or would like to play with their toys on their own. At this stage, too, infants vocalize using cooing sounds and they like you to react by repeating what you have heard back to them (reflecting). Reading to infants, and including them in the story, is a great way to communicate with them. At 6 months infants babble in a sing-song fashion repeating *Ma ma, Ha ha, Ba ba, Ga ga, Wa wa*. You can encourage and support this universal pre-speech babbling by reflecting back what you have heard in a higher pitched voice. Around about this age, too, infants love to play *peek-a-boo*, a game that involves you hiding behind your hands and suddenly peeking out. At around 8–10 months infants' babbling sounds begin to differ according to their country of origin. Having an awareness of cultural difference in how parents speak to their infant is important.

Use a soothing and calming tone when speaking to an infant

A soothing and calming tone when talking to the infant helps allay anxiety. Speak slowly, watch and wait for a response. Emphasize the vowels in the words you use, for example *Ooooh!, Aaaah!, Uuuu aaare sooo goood!* Aistear (NCCA 2009), the early learning curriculum, offers an excellent guide for adults to initiate, develop, and support communication skills when working with infants, toddlers, and young children. From 9 to 12 months infants might say 'mama' or 'dada' for the first time, and will communicate using body language. They pay even more attention to your words and try very hard to imitate you. They begin to express likes and dislikes with body language, nodding in agreement or wrinkling their nose with displeasure. They begin to communicate what they want by pointing, crawling, and gesturing. They cooperate when you are dressing them and make good progress with feeding themselves. They may not be walking but they can sit up, pull themselves up to stand, and they may be crawling or furniture walking. They recognize their own name and can obey simple instructions, such as *come to me* and *wave bye bye*. Reading to infants at this developmental stage is a wonderful way for them to learn more about themselves and the world around them.

Activity

Observe a young baby for about 10–15 minutes interacting with their mother/father/carer. Find out what age the baby is.

- What communication processes are taking place?
- Who initiates them?
- What does the adult do to enhance communication (e.g. proximity, position, gestures, eye contact, pause for response)?
- What parts of the baby's body are used in the communication?

Communicating with toddlers

Approach toddlers carefully, as they are often fearful and quite resistant

Developmentally, from 18 months to 2 years toddlers are walking and running. They use between 6 and 50 recognizable words and can put 2–4 words together to make a sentence (e.g. *Mama gone, all gone*). They can play alone content with toys for longer periods and engage in pretend play. At this stage, too, they can alternate between clinging and resistance to parents and are resentful of attention paid to other children. Toddlers can be resistant and fearful of new people, so approach them carefully using a calm and soothing voice. If you get no response, make another effort and wait for them to respond, keeping a distance of about a metre or slightly more away from them and observe what they are doing. In general, a toddler's communication may be indirect while they are engaged in an activity such as drawing or playing with toys.

Use the toddler's particular words for objects and actions

Become familiar with toddlers' particular words for objects and actions they are using so that you can support the communication process by reflecting back what they have said or done. This allows them to feel acknowledged and understood. Reflecting back is a useful communication tool to practise and develop when giving or receiving feedback to children. It lets them know that they have been heard and understood. Aistear (NCCA 2009) offers the following guidelines to support toddlers in their communication:

- name familiar objects and describe experiences;
- read, enjoy, and explore stories (these could focus on healthcare settings);
- use pretend play, music, and art activities.

Prepare toddlers for procedures just before they are about to occur

Break the procedure down into different steps and explain simply and honestly what you are going to do just before each step. Give the toddler time to respond before going on to the next stage. Offer praise and encouragement at each stage.

Activity

Drawing on your clinical practice experience, choose one simple procedure (e.g. taking a toddler's temperature) and one more difficult procedure (e.g. assisting a colleague in taking a blood sample from the toddler). Break down the procedure and identify the different steps for each procedure. At each stage, indicate what supportive communication strategies you use to progress to the next step of the procedure.

- How do you react to the toddler's distress if it presents?
- How do you react to your own distress and maintain clarity and focus?

Communicating with preschool children

At this stage, children are full of wonder, curiosity, and the desire to explore and create. They like to establish good relationships with adults and peers, and enjoy communicating with them. They are developing self-esteem and self-control while still somewhat unsure of themselves in new environments. They like to play with peers and alone. Through their play and exploration they develop concentration and a range of skills and competencies. They are learning to reason and solve problems and can, with the support and guidance of adults, further enhance their own learning. Preschool-age children enjoy stories, rhymes, music, and physical play and are becoming more independent. The confines of illness can frustrate these interests and abilities and can dampen their usual curiosity and playfulness.

Use play, puppetry, and storytelling

When considering how best to approach direct communication with this age group, you can look to props for assistance. Puppetry and storytelling can provide a safe external context for considering new and sometimes frightening facts. Many books are available that address issues around illness in a manner that gently approaches the issues children need to make sense of and understand. Taking the time to listen to children and their interests can often assist in the selection of an appropriate and effective story or puppet. At this stage, children have had contact with a fairly wide group of people and are sensitive to the authentic voice of the adult. They are quick to pick up tones of voice that may be infantilizing or patronizing to them. It is important that children feel secure in their relationships with adults and that they know adults are there to support them, treat them as individuals, and sensitively participate in their play.

Speak honestly using simple connected terms

Notwithstanding the growing vocabulary and verbal capacity of most preschool children, their ability to understand complex sentences, particularly in relation to the unfamiliar, should not be taken for granted. Be clear and honest in what you want to communicate. Think carefully about the core message you want to get across and the behaviour and response you want to get from the child. Children often ask questions by way of assisting them in understanding new situations. They like to feel comfortable and at ease wherever they are. In general, children settle in as they begin to establish relationships with adults and other children, and as they become familiar with their environment. As they learn to talk with adults on a one-to-one basis or in groups, children acquire more knowledge and understanding of the world around them.

Allow the child to have choices, as appropriate

When ill, children experience a vast array of different feelings, often new and uncomfortable ones. Use the language of feelings to assist them in adjusting to their new situation. *I feel scared today because _____ I was sad yesterday when _____.* Encourage young children to draw as well as talk about their fears, what they like, what they don't like. Provide props where possible. Help the child to identify what they can do as well as suggesting ways around what they cannot do. Make the communication lighthearted and be clear. Adjusting to the restrictions of healthcare environments can be a challenge for 3- to 4-year olds. Think of ways in which you can provide choice for them in respect of procedures you need their cooperation with. Where possible, create choices in activities, toys, books, and healthcare procedures (e.g. choosing different coloured plasters). When a child feels they have some control of their environment, they are more relaxed and more likely to be cooperative.

Prepare preschoolers about one hour before procedures

Prepare 3- to 4-year-olds about one hour before procedures. At this stage in their development, children do not have a secure grasp of time. They are not usually able to hold the logic and import of instructions for any length of time and they do not fully understand the implications of procedures if given details too early. While the concept of time is difficult for children to understand, activities such as daily routines, listening to 'once upon a time' stories, talking about various events, festivals, and other special occasions should help them develop an awareness of time. It is helpful for you to spend time preparing yourself carefully so that you are ready for the unexpected questions, the uncertainties and fears that may arise. Where relevant, help children to reflect on what has happened before, be open to questions with a genuine desire to answer, and minimize the unknown by accentuating the familiar. Planning is important and is enhanced when you have been observant of the child in advance and when you have had the opportunity to talk with other adults who may know the child better than you.

Activity

As a healthcare worker, self-awareness is crucial to learning and therefore you must identify what skills you have and what skills you need to develop for working with young children.

- Think about how relaxed you are in the presence of preschool children.
- Recall examples of how you have facilitated developmentally appropriate play with a 3- or 4-year-old child and identify what skills you used.
- Provide examples of how you did support or could support this play, for example by reflecting back and engaging in pretend play.
- Consider how comfortable you are with long silences.
- How do you maintain positive and supportive communication with a young child undergoing painful procedures? Give examples.

Communicating with school-age children

The age range here is very wide, including competent older children who can often be communicated with as young adults alongside younger children who need more careful consideration. Younger school-aged children may cope with healthcare experiences by exhibiting behaviour more appropriate to the preschool child. In such instances, it is important to recognize this as a coping strategy and to be respectful of it while at the same time trying to move beyond it by treating the child in an age-appropriate way. On the other hand, older school-age children may want to be treated as 'grown-ups' and not like a baby. It can be a difficult challenge to balance the need to respect the different styles of this age range while at the same time looking out for ways in which to make the overall experience one that is manageable and that limits fear and uncertainty. Older children may not want to ask questions in an effort to appear to be managing but good nursing will recognize this coping strategy and find ways to communicate answers to these unasked questions.

Use diagrams, illustrations, and books

At this stage in their development, most children will be able read, although younger children may have only a limited ability and picture books continue to be helpful. Diagrams of procedures, likely instruments and settings to be encountered can be very useful props for leading discussion at this stage. With 4- to 6-year-olds, it is still helpful to use props by way of illustrating certain procedures and to show them what they may look like following a procedure.

Allow child to express feelings

It is important for children's positive development and well-being that they express their feelings in useful and meaningful ways. The opportunity for this can be provided through a variety of different communication methods. Often just being present, and chatting in an informal way, can create an environment where a child may begin to feel sufficient trust to raise a concern or fear. It is crucial for you to be aware that this can happen and be quick to pick up these communication opportunities.

Use third-party stories to elicit desired information

Direct questioning, careful observation, and informal chatting may not always provide you with the information necessary. It is useful to use stories that create an opportunity for leading questions that give insight into the views of children, such as *What if that were you _____? How might you _____? Do you think that _____?* This less direct approach often allows children to voice concerns or ask questions they might not otherwise do.

Allow child to ask questions and allow adequate time for answering

Time is important. It is unfair to children to create a space for conversation about feelings or for questions without allowing the time to offer them a listening ear and a careful response. Children are less likely to understand the pressures of work and this, too, may have to be explained.

Prepare child a few days in advance of procedures

The older the child, the more able they are to prepare in advance of a procedure and the more likely they are to take the time to think things through in greater detail and ask more searching questions. Be as honest with this age range as you think you can but keep an eye to signs that they have sufficient knowledge. Do not complicate things – sometimes an apparently difficult question can be answered at face value.

Conclusion

This chapter has outlined some considerations and methods that can be used to support you and your communication with young children and their parents. There are also good books and articles referenced for you to study further. Communication is a skill that you can improve with practice. When working with children who are ill, our natural instinct is to protect them from worries and stresses and this sometimes causes us to avoid talking with them about their illness. The challenge is to find ways to communicate that are age-appropriate, culturally sensitive, and contextually bound. Using play with children as a tool to enhance communication is beneficial at every stage during childhood. Being self-aware is central to all communication and it is good practice to reflect on how you are giving and receiving information.

Key messages

- Communicating positively with children of all ages is a skill that needs to be continuously improved. Self-awareness is central to this improvement and all communication with infants and young children.
- Developmentally appropriate communication strategies should be used when working with children in all healthcare settings.
- Being culturally sensitive in your communication with children and their families is essential.

References

Alderson, P. (1993) European charter of children's rights, *Bulletin of Medical Ethics*, 92: 13–15.

Corlett, J. and Twycross, A. (2006) Negotiation of parental roles within family-centred care: a review of the research, *Journal of Clinical Nursing*, 15(10): 1308–16.

Coyne, I. (2006) Consultation with children in hospital: children, parents' and nurses' perspectives, *Journal of Clinical Nursing*, 15(1): 61–71.

Coyne, I., Hayes, E. and Gallagher, P. (2009) Research with hospitalised children: ethical, methodological and organisational challenges, *Childhood*, 16: 413–28.

Fenwick, J., Barclay, L. and Schmeid, V. (2001) ' Chatting': an important clinical tool in facilitating mothering in neonatal nurseries, *Journal of Advanced Nursing*, 33: 583–93.

Hughes, M. (2007) Parents' and nurses' attitudes to family-centred care: an Irish perspective, *Journal of Clinical Nursing*, 16(12): 2341–8.

Irish Association of Hospital Play Staff and Children in Hospital Ireland (IAHPS/CHI) (2000) *The Hospital Playlink – Play in Hospital . . . Everywhere Series*. Dublin: Children in Hospital Ireland.

Lao Tzu (Chinese Taoist Philosopher, founder of Taoism, wrote 'Tao Te Ching' (also 'The Book of the Way'). 600 BC-531 BC)

Levetown, M. (2008) Communicating with children and families: from everyday interactions to skill in conveying distressing information, *Pediatrics*, 121: e1441–60.

McPherson, A. (2010) Involving children: why it matters, in S. Redsell and A. Hastings (eds) *Listening to Children and Young People in Healthcare Consultations*. Oxford: Radcliffe Publishing.

National Council for Curriculum and Assessment (NCCA) (2009) *Aistear: The Early Childhood Curriculum Framework*. Dublin: NCCA.

Office of the Minister for Children and Youth Affairs (OMCYA) (2006) *Diversity and Equality Guidelines for Childcare Providers*. Dublin: OMCYA.

Petrie, P. (2011) *Communication Skills for Working with Children and Young People*. London: Jessica Kingsley.

Ricks, F. and Charlesworth, J. (2003) *Emergent Practice Planning*. New York: Kluwer Academic/Plenum Publishers.

Riley, A.W. (2004) Evidence that school-age children can self-report on their health, *Ambulatory Pediatrics*, 4(4): 374–6.

Scott-Ricci, S. and Kyle, T. (2008) *Maternity and Pediatric Nursing*. Philadelphia, PA: Lippincott Williams & Wilkins.

United Nations (1989) *United Nations Convention on the Rights of the Child*. Geneva: United Nations.

Zeskind, P.S. (1983) Cross-cultural differences in maternal perceptions of cries of low and high risk infants, *Child Development*, 54(5): 1119–28.

3 Communicating with young people

Debbie Fallon

After working through this chapter, you will have considered whether communication with young people provides an extra challenge to nurses, and whether it requires an additional set of skills. Throughout, you should ask yourself whether young people's communication needs are different to those of any other groups, and if so, in what ways.

> ## Learning outcomes
>
> By the end of this chapter you should be able to:
>
> 1. Describe the origins of the concept of adolescence
> 2. Consider the transition experiences of young people in contemporary society
> 3. Appreciate the impact of biological, psychological, and social factors that influence communication experiences of young people
> 4. Identify the factors that potentially can help or hinder effective communication between young people and health professionals

Introduction

In accordance with the Nursing and Midwifery Council (NMC) and An Bord Altranais (ABA) Standards for Nurse Education (ABA 2005; NMC 2010), all qualified nurses should be competent to communicate safely and effectively with patients and their families regardless of the skills that the patient or family may have. For the young patient, effective communication clearly facilitates understanding, but it can also be therapeutic, impacting on physiological processes such as pain perception or behaviours such as compliance with treatment through the cultivation of trust and confidence in the care provider.

A key consideration in communication for children's nurses is the developmental age and stage of the patient, and where they are in terms of the transition from childhood to young adulthood, since this inevitably impacts not only on their understanding but also on the dynamics of communication in what can be a stressful healthcare environment. Interactions may begin as dyadic exchanges between healthcare providers and parents with children as bystanders. This should progress to a triadic model of communication where the young person plays an active role in information exchange and decision-making.

Young people as a distinct client group

Adolescence is now understood to be a distinct stage of human development, and it is often discussed in terms of specific age ranges. The Americanism 'teenager' is, perhaps, the most popular lay description, where the age range 13–19 years (the 'teens') is the marker. The age range 10–19 years is used by the United Nations Children's Fund (2011: 6) to define adolescence, referring to the second decade of an individual's life, although the 'manifest gulf in experience that separates younger and older adolescents' is acknowledged, with the further suggestion that it is useful to consider the second decade of life in two parts: early adolescence (10–14 years) and late adolescence (15–19 years). While 'adolescent' is the preferred term in medicine and psychology, it is something of an unpopular term in sociological literature, since it is thought to invoke medical connotations, and the term 'young people' is used instead. Both terms will be used in this chapter to reflect the influences of the two disciplines.

Reflection point

- What are the key points of transition in a young person's life?
- What activities are restricted by age?
- Reflect on your own experience to identify the key points of transition in your life. Make a brief bullet-point list.

Transitions

Coleman (2011) suggests that contemporary understandings of adolescence are rooted in notions of transition. Transition in this context relates to an accumulation of biological, psychological, and social experiences that help to move an individual along a continuum from dependence to independence. Sometimes, these changes are described in terms of 'tasks' of adolescence (Christie and Viner 2005). In parallel with this journey from childhood to adulthood, children's nurses might consider the transition from paediatric to adult health services for those with long-term conditions.

In biological terms, although behavioural traits such as mood intensity and irritability, or late night wakefulness and early morning fatigue are often identified as being typical of adolescence (Buchanan *et al.* 1992; Coleman 2011), recent research has reiterated the important influence of hormonal changes on these behaviours

(Coleman 2011). Although the biological features of pubertal timing are perhaps the most obvious marker for the onset of adolescence, puberty should only be regarded as one element of transition to adulthood. Difficulties are associated with measurement (Walvoord 2010), and changes occur at different points for boys and girls (United Nations Children's Fund 2011). It is now acknowledged that the age at which puberty occurs across the population is decreasing (Walvoord 2010; Coleman 2011). Some suggest that the age of pubertal onset has declined by three years over the last two centuries, indicating that some individuals may reach puberty in their first decade.

Psychological evidence had suggested that the brain is completely mature by puberty, but research now highlights that development and maturation continue into the twenties (Johnson *et al.* 2009; Steinberg 2010). This means that while many young people may have the physical characteristics associated with an adult physique, their psychological development in terms of reasoning, self-control, and emotional regulation may occur much later in life. This may explain externalizing behaviours such as risk-taking (Darlington *et al.* 2011). These ideas, particularly the possible connections between neurological development and judgement, have caught the attention of the media and begun to shape public policy debates (Johnson *et al.* 2009). This is important because, as Bellis *et al.* (2006) suggest, the failure to recognize the increasing gap between physical and social development, or to develop young people socially in line with this, has been the root of many public health challenges.

Activity

Steinberg (2007) suggests that renewed interest in neurological maturation seeks to answer the question, 'Is risk-taking in young people both biological and inevitable?'

Why is this an important question for children's nurses to consider?

Take 15 minutes to make some bullet-point notes in response. (It may help to talk to colleagues, young people, and adults older than you to prompt different perspectives.)

A young person's transition to adulthood is further complicated by social inconsistencies and variations in the law relating to minimum age thresholds for activities such as babysitting, marriage, voting, joining the armed forces, consenting to medical treatment, buying cigarettes and alcohol, and leaving formal education. Such variations make defining young people's responsibilities and rights problematic both legally and socially, raising questions about why they might be considered to be old enough to engage in one action but not old enough to engage in another. Of course, the accepted age for some activities varies even more markedly across the globe. For example, in Iran the age of majority for females is 9 years (United Nations Children's Fund 2011).

Activity

Margo *et al.* (2006) argue that young people are living 'accelerated lives' in which emotional and social milestones are passed at younger and younger ages.

- Which of these are welcomed by society and which are seen as a cause for concern?
- What are the reasons for this?

Take 15 minutes to complete the following table:

Welcomed by society	Cause for concern	Why?

Theoretical approaches to adolescence

The difficult issues and stresses that young people face and the value they add to society have recently been acknowledged in Irish and UK health and social policy (Health Service Executive 2002; Department for Education 2011). However, in Western society adolescence as a stage of life is still considered to be troublesome by some. The language or 'discourse' that frames discussions about adolescence often includes elements of risk-taking, conflict or rebellion, and this has the potential to influence adolescents' experience as consumers of health care, including their communications with healthcare professionals.

Biology, psychology, and sociology

Professionals in health and social care draw upon a collection of theories of adolescence from biology, psychology, and sociology. Some of these ideas (the rebellious teenager and the malign peer group) have a long history but have endured despite less relevance today. Coleman (2011) suggests that many ideas in contemporary psychology were influenced by an 1882 Princeton Review that introduced the notion of heightened 'storm and stress' in adolescence. This stage of life has since been perceived as a time of crisis characterized by emotional unsteadiness, unreasonable conduct, and lack of enthusiasm. Rebellion, risk-taking, and non-conformity (Griffin 1997; Coleman 2011) and notions of a 'general concept of invincibility' (East *et al.* 2007) have subsequently emerged as almost universal features in theories of adolescence.

Negative stereotypes

Demos and Demos (1969) highlighted how adolescence came to be viewed as a time of change and conflict (following social anxiety about decreasing parental authority and the growing negative influence of the peer group at a time when young people began to socialize away from the home). Undoubtedly, the notions of the rebellious adolescent and the malign peer group have persisted in the guise of unhelpful stereotypes. The media constantly engages in sensational reporting of incidents involving a minority of adolescents, portraying them as being representative of the whole age group. When risk-taking and novelty-seeking are accepted as 'hallmarks' of typical adolescent behaviour (Kelley *et al.* 2004), such negative stereotypes of anti-social and sexually promiscuous adolescents are reinforced (Spence 2005). Conflict then becomes a central feature of communication because risk-taking and rebellion are put forward as the default position of young people.

Activity

Watch the news, a soap opera or a contemporary drama on TV, and read a newspaper – how are adolescents portrayed in the media?

Make notes in response to the following questions:

- Is the behaviour that you observe from these sources attributed just to the individuals in question or is it generalized to all adolescents?
- What are the responses of adults (and especially professionals where relevant) to these reports?
- How do they speak about and to the young people?
- What kind of impact could these images have on the lives of young people?

You may have identified how the images promoted in the media exert an immediate impact in terms of the attitudes of adults towards young people. For example, older people may fear young people. Some adults may express disdain for young people's behaviour (lazy students!). The images also have the potential to misrepresent social norms, promoting unattainable celebrity looks or lifestyle, which can result in low self-esteem.

The message for children's nurses

When communicating with young people, it is important to remain aware that these ideas have been so successfully integrated into the mainstream that they are often accepted as the 'natural facts' of adolescence. While 'storm and stress' may be more likely to occur during adolescence than any other stage of development (Arnett 1999), it is not necessarily a universal adolescent experience. Indeed, this stage of life is relatively problem-free for most young people

(Coleman and Hagell 2007). The positive impact of the peer group on the development of a young person's social skills and their sense of self should also be acknowledged.

This can be difficult, since guidelines for working with young people, including the 5–19 Healthy Child Programme (Department of Health/Department for Children Schools and Families 2009) and the Irish Health Behaviour in School-aged Children (HBSC) Study (Department of Health and Children 2007), are clear that the main risks to adolescent survival include accidents (especially road traffic accidents), AIDS, early pregnancy, unsafe abortions, substance misuse (smoking, alcohol, and drugs), mental ill health, and violence. A significant proportion of health-promoting activity for adolescents focuses on the risk-taking cluster of alcohol, drugs, and risky sexual activity. Practitioners are drawn to the association between risk and behaviour (Millstein and Halpern-Felsher 2002) because of the concern about the immediate danger of such activities, but also because experimental behaviour might be habit-forming and cause further health problems in adulthood. Young people with long-term conditions are doubly disadvantaged, since they engage in risky behaviours to at least similar if not higher rates as healthy peers (Sawyer *et al.* 2007) but may experience greater adverse health outcomes as a result.

Activity

Think about health messages targeting young people. Consider the current approach to smoking reduction/cessation in the general population, which involves the use of explicit messages on cigarette packets:

Warning! Tobacco smoke can harm your children
Smoking seriously harms you and others around you
WARNING! Cigarettes are addictive
Smoking causes fatal lung disease

Answer the following questions:

1. Does the provision of information always lead to positive changes in the behaviour of the general population? If not, why not?
2. Which aspects of this approach might appeal to young people specifically?
3. How does this approach compare with the various multi-media approaches specifically aimed at young people regarding risky sexual activity?
4. How could smoking reduction/cessation campaigns be more effectively aimed at young people?

Nurses must strike a delicate balance, resisting the stereotypical view of risk-taking young people while remaining aware of the likelihood of them experiencing new social situations with a peer group independent of their parents or carers. These situations may include opportunities to experiment with smoking, alcohol or drugs, or to engage in sexual activity. Discussion of these issues requires careful navigation if effective communication channels are to be maintained and a negative impact on health avoided. This includes approaching the subject in a non-judgemental manner, avoiding blame or moralizing, and with appropriate respect and consideration of the young person's viewpoint.

Communicating with young people in the contemporary healthcare context

Children's nurses encounter young people across the spectrum of health status. The young people may be receptive or hostile to input, and they may actively seek their parents' involvement or prefer to exclude them. They may be carers for a family member (McAndrew *et al.* 2012). These interactions may take place in inpatient, primary care, home, clinic, school, college or other settings such as pupil referral units. The location and conditions provide a communication context and, as with adults, each young person will have individual health-related information needs.

A recent review of children's and young people's views of health professionals (Robinson 2010) identified a range of attributes and skills that were expected. Communication issues were fundamental to this, including being familiar, available, accepting, informed and informative, empathic, and able to ensure privacy and dignity. Little research has specifically considered nurses' communication with young people. Callery and Milnes (2012) explored the role of younger children communicating with nurses, and other studies have focused on school health (Chase *et al.* 2006), but most research in this area has considered young people's concerns about their role in medical consultations whether in hospital or primary care (e.g. Mappa *et al.* 2010; Robinson 2010; Duncan *et al.* 2011; Helitzer *et al.* 2011). The identification of factors that help or hinder effective communication (e.g. Beresford and Sloper 2003) and the role of the young person in the communication dynamic (Tates and Meeuwesen 2001; Tates *et al.* 2002a, 2002b; van Staa 2011) have also emerged as key issues. Factors identified as hindering communication with medical staff included negative attitudes towards young people, and a focus on parents or the medical condition with too little interest in how the illness impacted on the young person's day-to-day life, school or emotional wellbeing. The type of information requested also hindered communication, such as when it was of a sensitive nature or revealed poor adherence or risky activity (Beresford and Sloper 2003).

In terms of the communication dynamic, van Staa's (2011) study of triadic communication revealed that the young person's contribution to the discussion was limited, despite both their desire and their feelings of competence to be regarded as partners in their own care. This was because doctors controlled the turn-taking, and parents tended to 'fill the gaps', leading van Staa (2011: 455–6) to conclude that young people were more likely to act as 'bystanders' in the consultation because 'their participation was neither requested nor encouraged'. Crucially, Robinson's (2010) review identified that the same broad messages had been repeated to professionals over the last decade.

Activity

Think for a few minutes about what you have just read and answer the questions below. Make some bullet-point answers.

- What opportunities are available to children's nurses to get to know a young patient?
- How might an interaction between a nurse and a young person differ from a medical consultation?
- What might prevent opportunities being seized?

There are some differences in the context of communication on which children's nurses could capitalize. For example, unlike a medical consultation in primary care where there is likely to be a substantial gap between appointments, the young person in hospital is likely to see a team of children's nurses 24 hours a day for the duration of their admission. If they are being visited at home, they are likely to be more confident in their own environment and with the support of their family, and they are likely to be visited on a regular basis until nursing support is no longer required. This is important because lack of familiarity can be a barrier to effective communication (Beresford and Sloper 2003), and children's nurses should make the time and opportunity to build a rapport with the young person. Nurses are also generally perceived to be less powerful than doctors and, therefore, more approachable (Tates et al. 2002b). This places you in a unique position to facilitate effective communication not only with the young person and their family, but across the whole team, for example by reassuring them that doctors are approachable and available to answer their questions, and relaying to the medical staff that the young person is wary of them when this is the case. In terms of your role in an initial medical consultation, you are perhaps just as likely to be a bystander as the young person, observing the exchange between the parent, doctor, and young person. However, a key role for you is to provide an opportunity for discussion once the consultation has ended: an opportunity to clarify issues for the family and to gain an appreciation of what has been understood.

A potential barrier to effective communication shared by doctors and children's nurses is the issue of confidentiality. Nurses are guided in matters of confidentiality by the NMC (2008a, 2008b) and ABA (2000) (Table 3.1).

One of the most complex tasks for children's nurses is the negotiation of a young person's confidentiality while maintaining the confidence of the parent. In a study of primary care providers, Helitzer et al. (2011) found that although these professionals acknowledged the importance of having a parent as part of a collaborative team, based on an overarching belief that adolescents engage in risky behaviours, they prioritized the privacy concerns of their young patients. In contrast, Mappa et al. (2010) found that only 23 per cent of clinicians routinely asked adolescents if they wanted to be seen alone (due to time constraints or perceptions that it was not necessary). This highlights a common difficulty for young people – whether they will be afforded some time to discuss issues privately.

Table 3.1 Confidentiality guidance for nurses

NMC (2008a)	An Bord Altranais (2005: 5)
Work within the legal frameworks of the country in which you are working to hold and share information, being mindful of your duty to protect children and young people from harm and to co-operate with other members of the team in order to provide safe and effective care	Any circumstance which could place patients/clients in jeopardy or which militate against safe standards of practice should be made known to appropriate persons or authorities
Share information that is required for safe practice and to safeguard children and young people in a sensitive and proportionate manner	Information regarding a patient's history, treatment and state of health is privileged and confidential. It is accepted nursing practice that nursing care is communicated and recorded as part of the patient's care and treatment
Work with children and young people to assist them in talking openly to others and sharing their own information	Professional judgement and responsibility should be exercised in the sharing of such information with professional colleagues
Where consent to share information is not given, you must decide and justify your decision to share the information or to withhold it	The confidentiality of patients' records must be safeguarded
Seek advice from your manager or experts in the field when you are unsure whether to share information	In certain circumstances, the nurse may be required by a court of law to divulge information held. A nurse called to give evidence in court should seek in advance legal and/or professional advice as to the response to be made if required by the court to divulge confidential information
Ask the child/young person how they want you to communicate sensitive information	The nurse must uphold the trust of those who allow him/her privileged access to their property, home or workplace
When using technology such as mobile phones and email to communicate with children and young people, you need to balance the benefits against the risk of breach of confidentiality	It is appropriate to highlight the potential dangers to confidentiality of computers and electronic processing in the field of health services administration
You should follow guidance, policy and legislation in doing this	

Young people are probably as interested in their health as are their parents, but their priorities may be different. Peer acceptance and conformity dominate early adolescence, but while parents might empathize with the young person's need to fit in with their peers, if a particular behaviour jeopardizes health parents will express concern, which could lead to conflict. Fitting in with peers will be a side issue for parents even if it is all-encompassing for the young person. Effective communication with young people requires navigation of these issues and might include balancing parental involvement with a young person's need for privacy – sometimes adopting a mediating role.

During any admission interview where the parent is present, children's nurses should be clear about why they are asking questions that may be sensitive or embarrassing, be able to explain the reasons for asking, phrase the questions clearly, and provide the young person with the opportunity to refuse to answer or answer at a later time if preferred, giving a rationale for this approach to the parent. This is basic good practice in assessment. Nurses should be aware if the presence of a parent is a source of interference, inhibiting information exchange, and modify their practice accordingly.

Children's nurses should be aware that withholding information can be a significant health risk both for the healthy adolescent and for the adolescent who has a condition that requires an element of self-management or compliance with a medication or dietary regime. Adolescents may employ strategies to withhold information such as telling only if asked, or providing partial information, and full disclosure may only occur if they feel that the consequences of not telling are too high (Marshall *et al.* 2005). You should consider the reasons why a young person might withhold information. Often adolescents regulate information in accordance with cues from parents, controlling information to prevent attention from being directed towards details that could jeopardize the parent's impression of them. In this way, they are able to avoid punishment or restrictions, or undue parental concern. Withholding information may also serve to protect friendships or a level of autonomy, since the young person is trying to balance safety issues with the preservation of the parent–adolescent relationship (Marshall *et al.* 2005). A further consideration may be that a young person is trying to protect a parent, for example if they care for a sick parent. This information may be sensitive, causing them embarrassment, or they may be worried that disclosure would bring unwanted attention from authorities (McAndrew *et al.* 2012). Bearing in mind that such responsibilities may be impacting on a young person's health, it is important that such situations are handled sensitively, and that the young person is reassured that help is available for them.

Application to practice

The success of much of this depends on key communication skills, such as making time (being available), being an encouraging listener, being aware of the tone, volume and speed of your own voice, and adopting positive body language. A trusting relationship is more likely to be established if the nurse exhibits qualities such as kindness, for example, noticing if a young person is distressed or uncomfortable, and responding appropriately (Kendal and Pryjmachuk 2011). It is important to recognize and acknowledge (rather than trivialize) stressors such as peer relationships, family worries or examination stress.

Engaging young people in everyday conversation is obviously a rewarding part of nurses' work, but this may not be easy if there is little understanding of the type of language or slang terms that young people use. While it is acceptable to ask a young person for clarification of terms that they have used, they would not welcome the sincere use of such terms by any health professional, since this is often a way of distinguishing themselves from older people and reinforcing their position in their own peer group.

It is acceptable for children's nurses to discuss some aspects of their own lives with young people (indeed this can help to engage a young patient), but careful self-monitoring should be involved. Bach and Grant (2010) make a useful distinction between professional and social behaviour when communicating with patients, emphasizing the importance of striking a balance between being professional and being over-involved. Part of this process involves knowing the difference between the disclosure of personal information that might be interesting but relatively insignificant, such as 'I went to a theme park this weekend and had a great time', and unhelpful disclosure about your personal life that may add to the burden of the young patient, cause them embarrassment or discomfort, or may glorify risky health behaviours (Petrie 2011: 89).

Activity

Think about shared language and meaning.

- What are the slang terms currently being used by young people that you know?
- What do they actually mean?

It might be helpful to ask young people that you know. You might observe some of the information-controlling behaviour described above.

Social media

The rapidly expanding world of social media has provided a multitude of opportunities for communication, leading Lenhart *et al.* (2010: 5) to describe the internet as a 'central and indispensable element' in the lives of teenagers and young adults. Mobile phones are increasingly recognized as tools to improve young people's access to health care. For example, the use of SMS messaging (texting) to facilitate contact with services (Furber *et al.* 2011) provides opportunities for direct communication that improves engagement and retention, especially when used for coordinating appointments. Young people are usually particularly adept at using the technology that facilitates this type of communication, including computers, smartphones, and consoles that enable interactive gaming across the globe. Many have been surrounded by such technology since birth. Social media also presents young people with the opportunity for easy communication with each other, even during hospitalization, potentially providing feelings of wellbeing through connection with friends. Since hospitalization has the potential to destabilize important peer relationships (D' Auria *et al.* 2000), particularly if this is a regular occurrence, children's nurses should endeavour to facilitate such connections for young people where possible.

Of course, many healthcare professionals also use social media, which is why many educational and healthcare institutions have developed guidelines regarding appropriate use. You may receive requests from young patients to accept them onto your personal social media websites, or to accept an invitation from them to join theirs. This is an activity that puts the registration of a qualified nurse at risk and jeopardizes the potential for a student to join the register (NMC 2008b, 2009). This may be a difficult issue for you to navigate, but it is helpful to remember the difference between being friendly and being a friend (Petrie 2011) and to explain a refusal sensitively.

The transition to adult care

The effective transition from paediatric to adult care is recognized as an important area for development in current healthcare provision (Health Service Executive 2002; Department of Health 2006, 2008). Young people have a legal right to partic- ipate in decision-making processes alongside their parents, and this is an essential step in transition to adult care. However, van Staa (2011) argues that the current structure of consultations, the communication style employed, and the presence of parents hinder the effective involvement of young people. Children's nurses have a role to play in helping young people with long-term conditions to become effective partners in their own health care in preparation for the transition to adult services. This should be commenced in good time and include a joint consultation between the young person, their parents, and the adult and paediatric healthcare providers. There may be times when the young person is happy to relinquish the lead to their parents, perhaps if they are too ill or exhausted. However, van Staa (2011) suggests that healthcare providers should encourage young people to take the lead in communication, where appropriate, by initiating independent visits and modifying parental involvement.

Activity

This is an exercise to do at work. You may need to identify the relevant individu- als with whom to discuss these issues.

Identify the systems and structures that exist in your own workplace that help to facilitate a smoother transition for young people to adult services. Are young people involved in these processes?

Conclusion

Adolescence is a ubiquitous term in health care, but what it means to be an adoles- cent is influenced by biological, psychological, and social factors that each young person experiences in a unique way. Young people have a distinct set of health needs, but health policy tends to focus on risky behaviour. To provide individual- ized care, practitioners need to be mindful that their perceptions and expectations of young people are often shaped by powerful social and media discourses. Young people with long-term illness require support in the transition to adult services, particularly as the health landscape is changing with an emphasis on increasing participation. All of these issues potentially impact on the young person's experience as a consumer of health care.

Key messages

- Children's nurses need skills to engage young people in everyday conversation at a time when they may feel vulnerable or stressed.
- Young people are individuals with the right to clear, effective, two-way communication with nurses and other healthcare providers, though they are, for the most part, 'connected' to their parents. At times, parents' priorities may differ from those perceived by young people, and this has the potential for conflict.
- Children's nurses require skills to negotiate relationships between teenagers and adults while respecting the rights and trust of all parties. Children's nurses are well placed to help ensure effective communication between young people and the rest of the multidisciplinary team.

References

An Bord Altranais (ABA) (2000) *The Code of Professional Conduct for each Nurse and Midwife.* Dublin: ABA.

An Bord Altranais (ABA) (2005) *Requirements and Standards for Nurse Registration Education Programmes.* Dublin: ABA.

Arnett, J.J. (1999) Adolescent storm and stress, reconsidered, *American Psychologist*, 54(5): 317–26.

Bach, S. and Grant, A. (2010) *Communication and Interpersonal Skills in Nursing.* Exeter: Learning Matters.

Bellis, M.A., Downing, J. and Ashton, J.R. (2006) Adults at 12? Trends in puberty and their public health consequences, *Journal of Epidemiology and Community Health*, 60(11): 910–11.

Beresford, B. and Sloper, P. (2003) Chronically ill adolescents' experiences of communication with doctors, *Journal of Adolescent Health*, 33: 172–9.

Buchanan, C.M., Eccles, J.S. and Becker, J.B. (1992) Are adolescents the victims of raging hormones? Evidence for activational effects of hormones on moods and behavior at adolescence, *Psychological Bulletin*, 111(1): 62–107.

Callery, P. and Milnes, L. (2012) Communication between nurses, children and their parents in asthma review consultations, *Journal of Clinical Nursing*, 21(11/12): 1641–50.

Chase, E., Goodrich, R., Simon, A., Holterman, S. and Aggleton, P. (2006) Evaluating school based health services to inform future practice, *Health Education*, 106(1): 42–59.

Christie, D. and Viner, R. (2005) ABC of adolescence: adolescent development, *British Medical Journal*, 330(7486): 301–4.

Coleman, J. (2011) *Adolescence*, 4th edn. Hove: Routledge.

Coleman, J. and Hagell, A. (2007) The nature of risk and resilience in adolescence, in J. Coleman and A. Hagell (eds) *Adolescence, Risk and Resilience: Against the Odds.* Chichester: Wiley.

Darlington, R., Margo, J., Sternberg, S. and Burks, B.K. (2011) *Teenage Girls' Self-esteem is More than Skin Deep ... Through the Looking Glass.* London: Demos.

D'Auria, J., Christian, B., Henderson, Z. and Haynes, B. (2000) The company they keep: the influence of peer relationships on adjustments to cystic fibrosis during adolescence, *Journal of Pediatric Nursing*, 15(3): 175–82.

Demos, J. and Demos, V. (1969) Adolescence in historical perspective, *Journal of Marriage and the Family*, 3(4): 632–8.

Department for Education (2011) *Positive for Youth*. London: The Stationery Office.

Department of Health (2006) *Transition: Getting it Right for Young People*. London: The Stationery Office.

Department of Health (2008) *Transition: Moving on Well*. London: The Stationery Office.

Department of Health/Department for Children Schools and Families (2009) *Healthy Child Programme: From 5–19 Years Old*. London: The Stationery Office.

Department of Health and Children (2007) *The Irish Health Behaviour in School-aged Children (HBSC) Study*. Dublin: Department of Health and Children.

Duncan, R.E., Vandeleur, M., Berks, A. and Sawyer, S. (2011) Confidentiality with adolescents in the medical setting: what do parents think?, *Journal of Adolescent Health*, 49(4): 428–30.

East, L., Jackson, D., O'Brien, L. and Peters, K. (2007) Use of the male condom by heterosexual adolescents and young people: literature review, *Journal of Advanced Nursing*, 59(2): 103–10.

Furber, G.V., Crago, A.E., Meehan, K., Sheppard, T.D., Hooper, K., Abbot, D.T. *et al.* (2011) How adolescents use SMS (short message service) to micro-coordinate contact with youth mental health outreach services, *Journal of Research on Adolescence*, 48(1): 113–15.

Griffin, C. (1997) Troubled teens: managing disorders of transition and consumption, *Feminist Review*, 55: 4–21.

Health Service Executive (2002) *Best Health for Adolescents. Get Connected: Developing an Adolescent Friendly Health Service*. Dublin: National Conjoint Child Health Committee.

Helitzer, D.L., Sussman, A.L., de Hernandez, B.U. and Kong, A.S. (2011) The 'ins' and 'outs' of provider–parent communication: perspectives from adolescent primary care providers on challenges to forging alliances to reduce adolescent risk, *Journal of Adolescent Health*, 48: 404–9.

Johnson, S.B., Blum, R.W. and Giedd, J.N. (2009) Adolescent maturity and the brain: the promise and pitfalls of neuroscience research in adolescent health policy, *Journal of Adolescent Health*, 45(3): 216–21.

Kelley, A., Schochet, T. and Landry, C. (2004) Adolescent brain development: vulnerabilities and opportunities, *Annals of the New York Academy of Sciences*, 1021: 27–32.

Kendal, S. and Pryjmachuk, S. (2011) Helping young people with mental health difficulties, in S. Pryjmachuk (ed.) *Mental Health Nursing: An Evidence Based Introduction*. London: Sage.

Lenhart, A., Purcell, K., Smith, A. and Zickuhr, K. (2010) *Social Media and Mobile Internet Use amongst Teens and Young Adults*, PEW Internet and American Life Project. Washington, DC: PEW Research Center.

Mappa, P., Baverstock, A., Finlay, F. and Verling, W. (2010) Current practice with regard to 'seeing adolescents on their own' during outpatient consultations, *International Journal of Adolescent Medicine and Health*, 22(2): 301–5.

Margo, J., Dixon, P.N. and Reed, H. (2006) *Freedom's Orphans: Raising Youth in a Changing World*. London: Institute for Public Policy Research.

Marshall, S.K., Tilton-Weaver, L.C. and Bosdet, L. (2005) Information management: considering adolescents' regulation of parental knowledge, *Journal of Adolescence*, 28: 633–47.

McAndrew, S., Warne, T., Fallon, D. and Moran, P. (2012) Young, gifted and caring: a project narrative of young carers, their mental health, and getting them involved in education, research and practice, *International Journal of Mental Health Nursing*, 21: 12–19.

Millstein, S.G. and Halpern-Felsher, B.L. (2002) Judgements about risk and perceived invulnerability in adolescents and young adults, *Journal of Research on Adolescence*, 12(4): 399–422.

Nursing and Midwifery Council (NMC) (2008a) *Advice for Nurses Working with Children and Young People*. London: NMC.

Nursing and Midwifery Council (NMC) (2008b) *The Code: Standards of Conduct, Performance and Ethics for Nurses and Midwives*. London: NMC.

Nursing and Midwifery Council (NMC) (2009) *Guidance on Professional Conduct for Nursing and Midwifery Students*. London: NMC.

Nursing and Midwifery Council (NMC) (2010) *Standards for Pre-registration Nurse Education*. London: NMC.

Petrie, P. (2011) *Communication Skills for Working with Children and Young People*. London: Jessica Kingsley.

Robinson, S. (2010) Children's and young people's views of health professionals in England, *Journal of Child Health*, 14(4): 310–26.

Sawyer, S.M., Drew, S., Yeo, M.S. and Britto, M.T. (2007) Adolescents with a chronic condition: challenges living, challenges treating, *Lancet*, 369(9571): 1481–9.

Spence, J. (2005) Concepts of youth, in R. Harrison and C. White (eds) *Working with Young People*. London: Sage.

Steinberg, L. (2007) Risk-taking in adolescence: new perspectives from brain and behavioural science, *Current Directions in Psychological Research*, 16(2): 55–9.

Steinberg, L. (2010) A behavioural scientist looks at the science of adolescent brain development, *Brain and Cognition*, 72: 160–4.

Tates, K. and Meeuwesen, L. (2001) Doctor–parent–child communication: a (re)view of the literature, *Social Science and Medicine*, 52: 839–51.

Tates, K., Elbers, E., Meeuwesen, L. and Bensing, J. (2002a) Doctor–parent–child relationships: a 'pas de trois', *Patient Education and Counselling*, 48: 5–14.

Tates, K., Meeuwesen, L. and Bensing, J. (2002b) ' I've come for his throat:' roles and identities in doctor–parent–child communication, *Child: Care, Health and Development*, 28(1): 109–16.

United Nations Children's Fund (2011) *The State of The World's Children 2011: Adolescence – An Age of Opportunity*. New York: UNICEF.

van Staa, A.L. (2011) Unravelling triadic communication in hospital consultations with adolescents with chronic conditions: the added value of mixed methods research, *Patient Education and Counselling*, 82: 455–64.

Walvoord, E. (2010) The timing of puberty: is it changing? Does it matter?, *Journal of Adolescent Health*, 47: 433–9.

4 Using play and technology to communicate with children and young people

Frances Binns and Paula Hicks

The first part of this chapter deals with the importance of play as a means of communication and explores a variety of techniques and methods for communication and distraction. The chapter moves on to consider the use of technology as a medium for supporting information-provision and communication with children, young people and families. Web-based technologies which have particular relevance for children and young people are considered in detail.

Learning outcomes

By the end of this chapter you should be able to

1. Understand the value of play as a method to help children to communicate with health professionals
2. Develop resources to aid distraction and to help children to develop coping mechanisms during treatment
3. Understand how technology can augment and support communication processes and information provision for children, young people, and their families
4. Appreciate some of the challenges to be addressed when using Internet technologies in health care to communicate with children and young people

---

Introduction

Play is an integral part of a child's life. It plays a major role in children's development and acquisition of skills. As a means of expression, it is one way in which

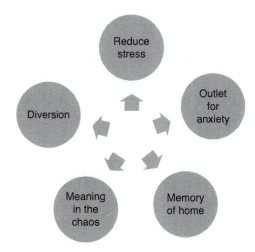

Figure 4.1 Ways in which communication through play can help

children can work through and explore feelings and emotions, enabling them to understand and cope with them. Play may, at first sight, appear to be simple and enjoyed only for its entertainment value. However, beneath the apparent simplicity lies a complexity in which ideas, understanding, exploration, and communication are pursued with vitality and developing skill. Play is a vital part of a child's life – an important means by which they can experience, interact, and connect with the world around them and thus develop physical, emotional, cognitive, and psychosocial skills that can enable an individual to exist in the world. It is a vital means by which children can express themselves.

Using play to address the negative consequences of being in hospital

Communication through play can help in at least five ways (Figure 4.1). It can reduce stress, provide an outlet for anxiety, offer a diversion from unpleasant treatment, bring meaning to the chaos of healthcare experiences, and keep alive the memory of home and all that is familiar and cherished.

Activity

Construct a table like that below. Imagine (or remember) being a child or young person in hospital, and try to think of some negative aspects of being in hospital together with ways in which play might have helped. Think about the issues in Figure 4.1. One example has been added to get you started.

Negative aspects of being in hospital	Ways in which play could help
Developmental regression (usually temporary)	Stimulation through familiar, age-appropriate games and activities

Hint: Try to see the left column from a child's point of view before thinking what practitioners could do to help.

You might have considered some of the following:

Play gives the child an outlet, a means of expression, a way to adjust to the stressful and frightening environment

Play gives the child a means of playing out fears of treatment, anger at having pain inflicted on them, and distress at being away from home

It provides the pleasure and comfort of doing ordinary things and playing with familiar play materials

Play can keep alive ideas of home and family

The child can play out meal times in the doll's corner, talk about family and pets through play, or make gifts or pictures for family members

Play removes some of the tension and formality of medical routines

It can fulfil the need for sympathetic interest and concern from a constant, familiar adult

Play can help a child to regain a sense of skill and achievement, counteracting unpleasant feelings of helplessness and dependence

Play can reassure a child that their body is still functioning

Play promotes normal growth and development

Play situations encourage children to make friends and to gain support from each other

Play can serve as a diversion to keep a child's mind off pain and treatments

The importance of play for children in hospital is highlighted in Ireland's 'Ready, Steady, Play' policy (National Children's Office 2004). The UK Department of Health (2003: 15) has set a clear standard for access to play therapy by children in hospital:

The use of play techniques should be encouraged across the multidisciplinary team caring for children, including in A&E, with play specialists taking a lead in modelling techniques that other staff can then adopt. The team should be able to offer a variety of play interventions to support the child at each stage in his or her journey through the hospital system.

Vignette   Maire

Maire is 4 years old. She has just arrived in the emergency assessment area following an accident at home. She has severe burns on her legs and will need to stay in hospital for treatment and dressings. Her pain is under control, but she is upset and uncooperative.

Activity

- How do you think that she might be viewing the situation? (Why is she upset and not cooperating?)
- How would you distract her while essential procedures are undertaken?

Take just five minutes. Don't worry if you struggle to answer this now. You can come back to it shortly.

There is a need for play every day, including evenings. Professional play specialists should be available to encourage and help nurses to play with children who are patients, helping the children to adjust to the potentially stressful experience of their stay in hospital.

Therapeutic play

Note that play is seen to be both a means of communication and a mode of therapy. It may be that play is simply a means for children to express their needs and desires. At other times, play may be used to affect a positive therapeutic outcome. Often, these are closely linked, since discovering a means of communication can be therapeutic itself. While there can be significant overlap, therapeutic play may be categorized as *non-directive play*, in which the therapist allows the child to play freely and takes the role of observer, or *directive play*, in which the practitioner engages actively in play activities. In both cases, it is usual for children to be allowed to start the interaction and choose the form of play, but the different approaches may be seen as the episode progresses.

Non-directive play

Non-directive play may take many forms:

- *Neutral play*: activity chosen by the child to allow a relationship to be built.
- *Regressive play*: the child plays at a lower developmental age level.
- *Projective play*: the child projects feelings, fears, and fantasies onto play materials.
- *Destructive play*: activity centres around destroying an object that has been constructed.
- *Social play*: the child plays cooperatively with other children (allowing for limitations of age and development).

- *Construction play*: use of play materials or purposeful activities.
- *Creative/expressive play*: the child portrays aspect of personality through a play or activity medium.
- *Socially acceptable activity for outlet of feelings*: using play to sublimate feelings.
- *Aggressive play*: activity used to express aggression.
- *Fantasy play*: imaginative play using fantasy themes.
- *Imitative play*: imaginative play that copies adult activities.
- *Stereotype play*: no purpose, repetitive.
- *Self-isolating play*: absorbed solely in activity – no contact with others.

In all of these, play and activities are used to provide a means for children to communicate their feelings – anger, loneliness, unhappiness, aspirations, fears, anxieties, hopes, preferences.

Directive play

Directive play is aimed more at assessment, intervention, and therapy. Activities are more likely to be directed by the practitioner. Again, varied forms and focuses are possible:

- *Diagnostic assessment*.
- Play to allow *regression*.
- *Developmental training*: providing toys suitable for the developmental stage or specific remedial toys to increase acquisition of skills.
- *Socializing activities*.
- *Socially acceptable activities for outlet of feelings*: activities provided by the therapist to sublimate the feelings of the child.
- *Satisfying dependency needs*: activities to allow the child to be dependent on the therapist.
- *Projective play*: to explore feelings.
- Play to increase *independence*.
- Play as a means of *non-verbal communication* for the child.
- *Neutral play*: to establish a relationship.
- *Constructive play*: to promote a feeling of being constructive and purposeful.
- *Creative* or *expressive* play.
- Play to improve the child's *confidence or self-image*.
- *Aggressive play*: to allow an outlet for aggressive feelings.
- *Imitative play*: learning, creating, expressing.
- *Passive play*: to allow the child to feel more secure so they can explore problems further at another time.

Activity

Look at Figure 4.2. Many aspects of directive and non-directive play are listed. See if you can identify which of these fit with both approaches and could be recorded in the overlapping area between the groups.

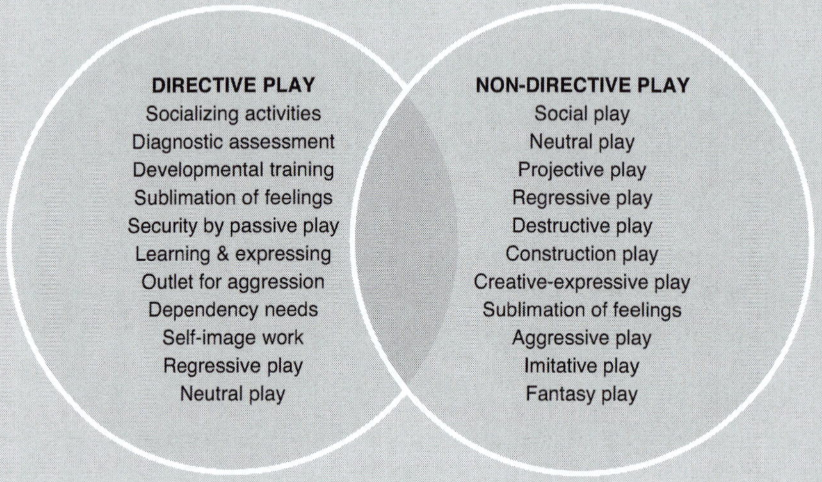

DIRECTIVE PLAY
Socializing activities
Diagnostic assessment
Developmental training
Sublimation of feelings
Security by passive play
Learning & expressing
Outlet for aggression
Dependency needs
Self-image work
Regressive play
Neutral play

NON-DIRECTIVE PLAY
Social play
Neutral play
Projective play
Regressive play
Destructive play
Construction play
Creative-expressive play
Sublimation of feelings
Aggressive play
Imitative play
Fantasy play

Figure 4.2 Directive and non-directive play

You probably found that the type of play is of less importance than the intention of the practitioner. Learning some basic skills is easy, and even a small repertoire of play strategies would enhance an individual nurse's ability to impact positively on the quality of their communication with children.

Communicating with children: preparation for hospital and for painful procedures

Children who are not prepared for admission to hospital may show adverse behaviour such as developmental regression, anxiety or fear (though usually only in the short term). Behaviour can be disturbed (sometimes in the longer term) if the child feels unable to cope with stressful experiences. Preparation through play is intended to help children to understand what is going to happen to them so that they may cope better. Part of this involves work to eliminate misconceptions and fantasies – often willingly exaggerated by school friends. If preparation through play can enhance a child's confidence, it may also help them to feel in control and relaxed through otherwise stressful events. It may, for example, help them to overcome the paralysing effect of fears and anxieties (such as fear of injections). Effective preparation before procedures can reduce emotional trauma after the procedure, which in turn accelerates recovery and reduces the amount of time spent in hospital.

Vignette   Matthew

Matthew, aged 7 years, has malaria. He hates injections and blood transfusions. He worries all the time about being sick and having to come to hospital so often for treatments. It is time for his treatment again.

Activity

Think how you would deal with Matthew. The following questions might help you to formulate your plan:

- What can be done in preparation for his visit?
- What are the key problems from Matthew's perspective?
- Are there information needs?
- Are there needs for anxiety-reduction? Distraction?
- Is this all going to happen again next time?

Distraction therapy

Distraction therapy is a way of helping a child to cope with a painful or difficult procedure. The aim is to take the child's mind off the procedure by concentrating on something else that is happening. There are various methods of distraction therapy – some very simple to implement, and others that need more practice (Table 4.1). Ideally, distraction techniques should be practised 5–10 minutes before a procedure begins so that the child has the chance to become familiar with them. Each of these strategies may be implemented in different ways, depending upon the age, developmental stage, and state of health of individual children and young people.

Activity

Pick a pair of activities that are closely linked (for example, 'blowing bubbles' and 'rhythmic breathing'). Decide if one or other is better for younger or older children.

For each activity, think of a practical means to implement the distraction. Remember, focus on distraction as a means of effective communication to achieve a benefit for children and young people. It's not just for fun.

Table 4.1 Selected distraction techniques

Treasure box A box with small gifts or toys that can be given to the child during or after their procedure has finished	**Choices** Let children have choices if any are possible	**Step by step** Increase a child's understanding by explaining each step of the painful procedure and what to expect
Blowing bubbles Relaxes children by slowing and deepening the breathing	**Rhythmic breathing** Help to relax a child by inducing rhythmic breathing	**Magic blanket** Endow a blanket with 'magic powers' for relaxation, comfort, and protection
Counting Have school-age children count during a difficult part of the treatment	**Music** Helps to soothe or distract, especially when children pick the music	**Singing** A child who has not become too afraid or anxious may be soothed with singing
Visualization (for older children or adolescents) Have the child imagine going to a favourite place, talking with someone special, etc.	**Diversional talk** Talking about the weather, your last vacation, the child's family, or other things in a comforting, rhythmic voice can be calming	**Soothing touch** Rhythmic touch alleviates loneliness and fear and promotes relaxation
Magic glove (particularly for insertion of cannulae) Stroke each finger saying 'Now this finger will be numb'	**Positioning** Hold younger children in a position that is most comforting and supportive for them	**Pop-up books, hide-inside books, musical books** Such books can promote mind-stimulation and distraction

Engaging in communication through technology

Children's and young people's use of technology

Children's use of information and communication technology (ICT) is embedded in their daily lives, with various estimates of around 75 per cent regularly using the Internet at school or at home for education and entertainment. Children enduring a chronic illness are, in respect of their use of ICT, no different to their peers. Its use to develop and maintain relationships is particularly attractive to children and young people, and they see ICT as an integral part of everyday life. Children and young people are becoming active participants in their health care and need healthcare agencies to provide access to appropriate information and communication resources.

Social networking and online environments allow customization of an individual space, as well as communication among users with the ability to share resources (e.g. pictures and videos). However, there are risks associated with these forms of communication, including the unintentional disclosure of personal information, bullying or harassment, and targeting of users by predators. The relative infancy of these new online resources, which have transformed the way in which children socialize, play, create, and share, means that there is little longitudinal research of the ultimate impact that the technologies will have on society as a whole.

Psychological background

Recent research has found that social media technologies that children and young people use on a regular basis can combat some of the psychological difficulties associated with chronic illness. Examples of these include discussion forums for patients and websites providing disease-specific information and support. Challenges that impact on a child's ability to cope socially, emotionally or physically include isolation, change in family dynamics, and loss of social interaction with peers. The stress and anxiety experienced by children and adolescents with chronic illness is higher than that found in their unaffected peers (Gupta *et al.* 2001). These problems, when related to illness, can hinder a child's treatment and recovery.

The importance of addressing psychosocial issues and the need to improve social support for children with chronic illness has been documented in the literature. Of particular relevance are the issues that long-term survivors may endure as a consequence of a stressful life experience such as a chronic illness. Global access to online resources and information can support children who do not know another child with similar difficulties. Such children may feel that their concerns are unique, and this isolates them from the wider community. Ellerton *et al.* (1996) found that children with a chronic condition reported smaller peer networks and more stress than healthy children. Perhaps not surprisingly, then, the opportunity to exchange information in existing social networks, in addition to establishing links with other children from the hospital community, has been shown to have tangible therapeutic benefits (Kazak *et al.* 1995). Anderson *et al.* (1989) reported that peers with the same medical condition helped facilitate other youngsters' adherence behaviours.

Activity

Select a chronic illness that is common in childhood. Search the Internet for related social networking or information exchange sites. Take a few minutes to analyse the sorts of information needs that are expressed and to appreciate the importance of mutual support.

- Why are such sites needed?
- Do they provide a different service to that offered by health services?

Technological interventions for children

Some of the technical initiatives to support children and young people include an array of technologies, including videos, CD-ROMS, websites, online support groups, and virtual reality headsets. These offer possibilities for providing information, distraction, and social support. Earlier initiatives addressed the use of video games to distract attention from painful procedures. These were followed by e-learning intervention programmes providing health-related information in an entertaining environment. Examples of these include 'What are blood counts?', designed to teach children about blood cells and the effects of chemotherapy (Peterson 1996), and 'Kidz with leukemia: a space adventure', designed to educate young people with leukaemia about the disease and its treatment (Dragone *et al.* 2002).

Activity

Take a few minutes to explore the 'Kidz with leukemia' site (http://www. kidzwithleukemia.com/). Focus on recognizing the communications strategies employed to transmit information and to encourage communication.

Email

One of the most frequently used Internet applications among organizations, universities, corporations, and private individuals' homes is email. It is a powerful connectivity tool that encourages networking among peers and facilitates the sharing of resources. Borowitz and Wyatt (1998) reported on a three-year study by a paediatric practice that offered free email as an option for communication with patients and their families. In total, 1239 emails were received from parents (81 per cent) and healthcare providers (19 per cent), and overall it proved to be an effective means for communication. Despite initial concerns of health professionals with regard to liability, confidentiality, and privacy issues, and worries about response times, health professionals were able to respond to emails in less than four minutes.

Blogs

Baum (2004) reported high levels of satisfaction with involvement in Internet support groups (web-logs or 'blogs'). Participants reported finding support in practical suggestions, improved relationships with their children, and establishing trusting relationships with other caregivers. Parents also found that participation in Internet support groups fostered hope. Researchers reported difficulties with establishing such Internet-based resources, the timing of when families are introduced in relation to the diagnosis, the need for a sufficient level of activity, and making the resources easy to use as important for the effectiveness of such interventions.

Web-based communities

The Internet offers much potential for empowering adolescents in coping with their illness as independently as possible. Examples include Starbright World, a private computer network for hospitalized children based in the USA. Research studies have illustrated the positive impact of a virtual environment on pain and anxiety for hospitalized children. Children involved in the network experienced less intense pain and anxiety (Holden *et al.* 1999, 2002). Starbright World also offers multimedia programmes on health care, and disease-specific information.

Áit Eile (Another World) is a virtual community developed by researchers at Trinity College Dublin and is currently based in hospital schools throughout Ireland. Maintaining access to education for young people with medical needs is an important aspect to this project. The activities offered by Áit Eile are designed to engage the children and to take their minds off their medical condition and treatment through entertainment and fun as well as fulfilling an important educational role. The Solas Project (Box 4.1) provides a virtual environment customized to the needs of children with cancer. Also developed in Trinity College Dublin, it provided a secure environment for children in isolation. Evaluation of the Solas Project concludes it has been of benefit to users and their families in the areas of communication, education, and entertainment.

Box 4.1 Solas – a virtual community for children with cancer

Solas is an online communications and creativity environment for hospitalized children. A particular target group of Solas are those whose conditions necessitate them being in protective isolation. Solas aims to empower children through facilitating communication, creative activities, and entertainment, which, it is hoped, will provide a temporary distraction from their illness. The services offered for communication include video-link, SMS texting, live chat, and email. Tools provided for creativity include Drumsteps (a musical composition tool), My Blog (which allows children to create multimedia blogs), Audio Stories (which provides audio books for users to listen to online), Art (which enables children to express their creativity through art), and Fun (consisting of a variety of single user games), and access to appropriate websites on a variety of topics.

Mobile technology

A text message (referred to technically as SMS – Short Message Service) is a technology standard that allows mobile telephone users to deliver short text messages. With the introduction of Smart phones, MMS (Multimedia Messaging Service) includes the sending of images, audio, and video over mobile networks. In a health context, mobile technology offers a low-cost solution to improving compliance and changing attitudes. It can be used to broadcast global reminders about medication and appointments, or positive health tips. As a two-way communication tool, texting may also be used to collect data from patients; for example, diabetic patients can text their blood results to the clinic. Children and young people are usually avid users of SMS and MMS modes of communication, and the potential for communication with them by this means should not be missed by health services.

Podcasts also provide an example of the potential for using mobile technology to deliver health-related messages. Podcasts have great impact potential and are time- and location-independent digital files.

Box 4.2   Pamphlets to podcasts

The Child and Family Information Group at Great Ormond Street Children's Hospital in London is one of the first to pioneer audio and video podcasts of information for patients and families. A variety of information sheets on diverse topics are already available to read online or download in PDF format. Supplementing these is a range of audio-visual podcasts that add more demonstrable clarity to certain topics. Examples of these include instructions for hand washing and preparing children for magnetic resonance imaging. It is also possible to reach a much wider audience through the use of mobile applications, as these podcasts can be downloaded and viewed on a variety of mobile devices (Moult et al. 2009).

The variety and quantity of health-related information available through the Internet can be overwhelming for both parents and children. Nettleton *et al.* (2004) conducted a qualitative analysis examining health-related Internet use by families with children with a chronic illness. Six distinct styles of Internet use were identified, ranging from problematic and reluctant Internet searchers to those who fully incorporated its use effectively. Families generally report a need to obtain health information from a reliable source and value support in this (Wainstein *et al.* 2006). One method that is considered credible by parents is obtaining information directly from hospital websites (Jury and Babl 2008; Khoo *et al.* 2008). It would be prudent for hospitals to take initiatives for the provision of such information (Sim *et al.* 2007), and Kind *et al.* (2004) urge leading children's hospitals to be at the forefront of providing health information within their own websites.

For a high proportion of adolescents, the Internet is their primary source of health-related information (Ybarra and Suman 2008). Skinner *et al.* (2003) recommend that healthcare professionals assist by supporting adolescents in accessing appropriate websites, incorporating computer-mediated communication as a means of connecting with adolescents, and helping adolescents to develop appropriate strategies to search for and evaluate the credibility of online health information. A further suggestion is that healthcare providers could use computer technology to engage with the marginalized and at-risk populations. Kyngas (2004) suggests that children and adolescents have embraced the Internet as a means of communication and provision of social support. It has become a valued component of psychosocial support for those children and adolescents with chronic health conditions. Ravert *et al.* (2004) note that 'adolescents with diabetes are adolescents first' and, as a consequence, may have psychosocial concerns that are not directly related to a health condition.

Ethical issues in providing technological solutions

Increasing demands from patients and parents alike to provide Internet services in hospitals raise many difficulties for hospitals. These include security, infrastructure, and resources. These are compounded by the lack of existing infrastructure and guidelines for Internet access by children in a hospital environment. Most websites include an acceptable use policy (AUP) for its users as a way of addressing inappropriate use. This ensures that users are aware of the boundaries within which they can use the online resource. Regular updating and revisiting of the AUP is required (with input from the users) to maintain acceptability and usability. The children's online protection policy (http://www.coppa.org) can form the basis for organizations' AUP. It has strict guidelines pertaining to the collection of data for children under the age of 13, which requires more stringent AUPs to be defined, and parental consent to be given in relation to any data collected about the children. Childnet International (http://www.childnet.com) is a charity established in 1996 to support both children and parents in keeping safe and getting the most out of online technology and to help to make the Internet a great place for children.

Technology as an empowering tool

Children want to have information and understand it, thus all available approaches to supporting this understanding and listening to the questions that arise from children should be explored. Technology has the potential to empower children to converse in a language that they understand. At a consultation, a child may not have sufficient time to think of questions about issues that cause them concern. Jaaniste *et al.* (2007) highlight the potential benefits for children and young adults when technological communication is exploited to provide them with accurate and age-appropriate information. It is possible to foster a child's trust, reduce uncertainty, and enhance confidence in their ability to cope. Each of these can potentially minimize distress and optimize treatment outcomes and recovery times. Benefits have also been seen for parents by easing the burden on them of what to tell their child, empowering them to support their child, and reducing their anxiety levels. For health professionals, the benefits accrued include making their role easier at the time of a medical procedure.

Conclusion

Play holds the potential to open channels of communication with children who find themselves in stressful, challenging situations. A wealth of strategies is available to children's nurses and other professionals to help facilitate communication with children and to distract them from uncomfortable or painful procedures. Nurses can learn many of these strategies to an adequate degree of competence, particularly when supported by professional play therapy staff. Regardless of the wide prevalence of ICT in modern life, its exploitation in health to date has been limited, and, in spite of the rapid growth in the use of the Internet for informa-tion and support, some socio-economically disadvantaged groups remain excluded from this support. The challenges to using technology are many, and as children and their families become more empowered users of our health services it is essen-tial that health professionals, too, become empowered and engage with these new technologies. Internet and e-health initiatives offer many solutions for empower-ing young patients to actively understand and influence their own health status.

Key messages

- Effective communication with children and young people sometimes requires alternative means and strategies. Both play and technology can bridge the divide between professionals and children/young people.
- Play is a form of two-way communication that is multi-faceted. Distraction is one of the most useful applications of play therapy, and a set of basic skills is within the grasp of all practitioners.
- The benefits of technology, particularly when Internet-based, must be consid-ered in the light of potential risks, but such risks can be managed effectively to allow exploitation of a powerful medium to the benefit of young people and their families.
- Increasingly, children, young people, and their parents look to Web2 technol-ogy for their information and communication needs. Healthcare professionals need to develop competence in this preferred mode of communication for in-formation and health messages to be received by the target audience.

References

Anderson, B.J., Wolfe, F.M., Burkhart, M.T., Cornell, R.G. and Bacon, G.E. (1989) Effects of peer-group intervention on metabolic control of adolescents with IDDM: randomised outpatient study, *Diabetes Care*, 3: 179–83.

Baum, L.S. (2004) Internet parent support groups for primary caregivers of a child with special health care needs, *Pediatric Nursing*, 30(5): 381–8, 401.

Borowitz, S.M. and Wyatt, J.C. (1998) The origin, content, and workload of e-mail consultations, *Journal of the American Medical Association*, 280(15): 1321–4.

Department of Health (2003) *Getting the Right Start: National Service Framework for Children. Standard for Hospital Services*. London: The Stationery Office.

Dragone, M.A., Bush, P.J., Jones, J.K., Bearison, D.J. and Kamani, S. (2002) Development and evaluation of an interactive CD-ROM for children with leukemia and their families, *Patient Education and Counselling*, 46(4): 297–307.

Ellerton, M.L., Stewart, M.J., Ritchie, J. and Hirth, A.M. (1996) Social support in children with a chronic condition, *Canadian Journal of Nursing Research*, 28(4): 15–36.

Gupta, S., Mitchell, I., Giuffre, R.M. and Crawford, S. (2001) Covert fears and anxiety in asthma and congenital heart disease, *Child: Care, Health and Development*, 27(4): 335–48.

Holden, G., Bearison, D.J., Rode, D., Rosenberg, G. and Fishman, M. (1999) Evaluating the effects of a virtual environment (Starbright World) with hospitalized children, *Research on Social Work Practice*, 9(2): 365–82.

Holden, G., Bearison, D.J., Rode, D.C., Kapiloff, M.F., Rosenberg, G. and Rosenzweig, B.S. (2002) The impact of a computer network on pediatric pain and anxiety: a randomised controlled clinical trial, *Social Work in Health Care*, 36(2): 21–33.

Jaaniste, T., Hayes, B. and von Baeyer, C.L. (2007) Providing children with information about forthcoming medical procedures: a review and synthesis, *Clinical Psychology: Science and Practice*, 14(2): 124–43.

Jury, S.C. and Babl, F.E. (2008) On-line health information from a children's hospital: user feedback, *Journal of Paediatrics and Child Health*, 44(6): 387–8.

Kazak, A.E., Boyer, B.A., Brophy, P., Johnson, K., Scher, C.D., Covelman, K. *et al.* (1995) Parental perceptions of procedure-related distress and family adaptation in childhood leukemia, *Child Health Care*, 24(3): 143–58.

Khoo, K., Bolt, P., Babi, F.E., Jury, S. and Goldman, R.D. (2008) Health information seeking by parents in the Internet age, *Journal of Paediatrics and Child Health*, 44(7/8): 419–23.

Kind, T., Wheeler, K.L., Robinson, B. and Cabana, M.D. (2004) Do the leading children's hospitals have quality web sites? A description of children's hospital web sites, *Journal of Medical Internet Research*, 6(2): e20.

Kyngas, H. (2004) Support network of adolescents with chronic disease: adolescents' perspective, *Nursing and Health Science*, 6(4): 287–93.

Moult, B., Stephenson, P., Geddes, N. and Webb, J. (2009) From pamphlets to podcasts: health information at Great Ormond Street Hospital for Children NHS Trust, *Journal of Visual Communication in Medicine*, 32(2): 43–7.

National Children's Office (NCO) (2004) *Ready, Steady, Play! A National Play Policy*. Dublin: NCO.

Nettleton, S., Burrows R., O'Malley, L. and Watt, I. (2004) Health e-types? An analysis of the everyday use of the internet for health, *Information, Communication and Society*, 7: 531–3 (special issue on E-Health: the use of information and communication technologies in the communication of health information and advice).

Peterson, M. (1996) What are blood counts? A computer-assisted program for pediatric patients, *Pediatric Nursing*, 22(1): 21–9.

Ravert, R.D., Hancock, M.D. and Ingersoll, G.M. (2004) Online forum messages posted by adolescents with type 1 diabetes, *Diabetes Education*, 30(5): 827–34.

Sim, N.Z., Kitteringham, L., Spitz, L., Pierro, A., Kiely, E., Drake, D. *et al.* (2007) Information on the World Wide Web – how useful is it for parents?, *Journal of Pediatric Surgery*, 42(2): 305–12.

Skinner, H., Biscope, S., Poland, B. and Goldberg, E. (2003) How adolescents use technology for health information: implications for health professionals from focus group studies, *Journal of Medical Internet Research*, 5(4): e32.

Wainstein, B.K., Sterling-Levis, K., Baker, S.A., Taitz, J. and Brydon, M. (2006) Use of the Internet by parents of paediatric patients, *Journal of Paediatrics and Child Health*, 42(9): 528–32.

Ybarra, M. and Suman, M. (2008) Reasons, assessments and actions taken: sex and age differences in uses of Internet health information, *Health Education Research*, 23(3): 512–21.

5 Communicating with parents of children with healthcare needs

Deirdre Kelleher

This chapter will focus on the communication needs of parents whose child has healthcare needs. Issues in relation to communication with parents of children with various healthcare needs will be outlined. Specific concerns related to differences between mothers' and fathers' communication needs in the therapeutic relationship will be explored. Strategies to achieve effective communication are suggested.

Learning outcomes

By the end of this chapter you should be able to:

1. Appreciate the issues faced by parents of children with healthcare needs
2. Discuss communication strategies that can enhance the relationship between parents and healthcare professionals
3. Identify the key differences and/or similarities in the communicative needs of mothers and fathers
4. Discuss the challenges health professionals face when communicating with parents of children with healthcare needs

---

Activity

A 9-year-old boy has been admitted to the surgical ward with burns and remains critically ill. His mother is present while the boy's father is at home with their other two children. The surgical team has just visited.

Consider the above and discuss with your colleagues. What information do you think the boy's mother will require as a parent?

Introduction

The publication of the Platt Report (Central Health Services Council 1959) acknowledged the importance of parental participation in the care of children in hospital. This research-based report reflected findings that separating children from their parents could have lasting negative effects on the overall development of the children. Parents, as children's carers, are now acknowledged to have expert knowledge and experience in the care of their children (Ball *et al.* 2012). Parents can detect nuances and changes in their children's behaviour and wellbeing, and can provide the emotional support required when a child is faced with an unfamiliar situation, such as being in hospital. Parents are increasingly becoming the primary caregivers in chronic childhood illness, thus effective communication between parents and professionals is instrumental in helping parents to cope with their children's healthcare needs (Swallow and Jacoby 2001; Hodgkinson and Lester 2002; Hopia *et al.* 2004). Ineffective communication in the absence of open and mutual negotiations between parents and professionals leads to misinterpretation over roles and expectations (Corlett and Twycross 2006). Parents want to be reassured that they are doing the best for their child – the most important thing in collaboration with parents in any healthcare setting is to make them feel good as parents (Ygge 2007). You need to be aware of the impact you can have when communicating with parents.

Vignette   Professional credibility

Luke, a 7-year-old boy, required an intravenous cannula for his medication. His mother Becky was present with him. Rachel, a staff nurse, came to insert the cannula and decided to site it in Luke's right arm. Becky advised her to put it in Luke's left arm but Rachel informed her that 'we always do it this way and we know what is right'. Rachel was unsuccessful in siting the intravenous cannula and had to finally insert it in Luke's left arm. Luke was crying.

Activity

- What issues may have prevented a favourable outcome in Luke's situation?
- Suggest how these issues may be addressed.

Family centred care

A collaborative approach between health professionals and parents in the care of their child requires good communication skills individual to each case (Hummelinck and Pollock 2006). A positive parent–health professional relationship is regarded as the foundation of family centred care (Fisher and Broome 2011). Family centred care is built on the foundation of dignity and respect, information-sharing, family partnership in care, and family collaboration (Griffin 2006). Good communication skills are required with parents and their child if such concepts are to be used to provide positive outcomes for both families and health professionals (Cone 2007). Effective communication is considered to be successful when there is a balance between neutral (giving information, opinions, and suggestions) and affective behaviours (building trust, showing respect, providing comfort) combined with emotional care and the delivery of consistent information (Shin and White-Traut 2005). Effective communication has also been linked to increased satisfaction with care, better compliance with prescribed treatments, and improved health outcomes by parents and their families (Howells and Lopez 2008; Ammentorp *et al.* 2010).

Reflection point

How can good communication skills contribute to the practice of family centred care?

You will need to assess each situational context before relying on subjective impressions and assumptions about parents' participation in the care of their child (Ygge and Arnetz 2004; Coyne 2008). Communication skills are a key element in the promotion of a positive relationship between the child's parents and health professionals. Parents who are empowered to voice their concerns and anxieties early in the communication process tend to be better informed, retain information more easily, and are more likely to be satisfied with the care provided (Howells and Lopez 2008; Fisher and Broome 2011).

Wales *et al.* (2008) found that parents reported good communication, appropriate information given, and a better provision of treatment options when their child was under the care of a single clinical team. Since it is likely that the decision-making process in relation to the care of a child will involve multiple health-care teams, the risk of poor communication is increased (Koshti-Richman 2008). Hawthorne *et al.* (2011) reported that parents felt that they had to repeat themselves to new staff, who gave the impression of knowing less than the parents, resulting in a lack of confidence in the ability of new staff to manage their child's care effectively. One strategy to minimize this risk is the creation of a collaborative climate between clinical teams, aiding effective communication between healthcare professionals and parents and their children. This strategy coupled with the recognition and acceptance of parents' views is paramount (Ygge and Arnetz 2004). Kowalski *et al.* (2006) found that parents identified the nurse as the person who provided them with the best source information about their child and the person who spent the most time explaining their child's condition.

Differences between the communication needs of mothers and fathers in the therapeutic relationship

It is recognized that parents are now more informed and more involved in their child's care and decision-making in health care than previously (Department of Health and Children 2009). While recognizing that the chief support system for both parents is the marital relationship, the quality of the relationship and support that the mother provides to the father has an important impact on the participation of fathers in their care-giving role (Simmerman and Blacher 2001; Devault *et al.* 2008; Pleck and Hofferth 2008).

Meeting the communication needs of fathers

Although it is important to recognize that fathers may have different communication needs to mothers, the prevailing culture continues to view childcare as predominately the mother's domain (Goldberg *et al.* 2009), and roles and responsibilities in relation to childcare continue to reflect traditional gender roles (Chesler and Parry 2001). Fathers today are expected to play a greater role in the care of their child in ways that go beyond the provider/protector role (Troilo and Coleman 2004). Differences in parental distress between mothers and fathers have been reported. Findings suggest that men are expected to be 'strong' and have the opportunity to return to work, which can shield them from some of the stressors (Chesler and Parry 2001; Mu *et al.* 2002; Fägerskiöld 2006). Fathers' sense of alienation may be increased when they are deemed to be secondary or peripheral in the participation of their children's care (Chesler and Parry 2001; Fägerskiöld 2006). Hill *et al.* (2009) suggest that fathers validated their peripheral role as a strategy either to support maternal coping or because of constraints arising from beliefs about gender and parenting roles. Board (2004) reported that the interpersonal rather than the physical dimensions of the healthcare setting were more stressful for fathers. Instructions that are repeated and reinforced enable fathers to participate in their child's care, while regular updates on the child's condition, including orientation to the changes that their child is likely to experience in the healthcare setting, are some of the strategies that may decrease fathers' stresses (Board 2004). It is important that fathers receive regular updates on the care of their child directly rather than second-hand via their partner (Fägerskiöld 2006).

Meeting the communication needs of mothers

Mothers continue to adopt the primary role in child-rearing and maternal stress can be increased by the number of tasks needed to be undertaken for the child, which may not be shared equally between the parents (Hodgkinson and Lester 2002). The positive attitudes of mothers towards their partner's role has been linked to greater involvement by fathers in the care of their child. However, the concept of 'maternal gatekeeping' (Allen and Hawkins 1999; Cannon *et al.* 2008) may have a punitive effect on fathers' involvement. Some mothers resist fathers' input and their adoption of new roles or new skills, even while desiring such participation (Chesler and

Parry 2001; Tiedje and Darling-Fisher 2003). This may be more pronounced when mothers view their role as central to their identity or have partners who are comfortable to remain in the background in family interactions (Pleck and Hofferth 2008). In contrast, maternal facilitative gatekeeping may encourage fathers in their interaction with their child and create opportunities for them to gain experience in the child's care, thus increasing collaboration between parents (Cannon *et al.* 2008). Fathers view partner support as important and their involvement in their child's care is influenced by their partner's preferences (Board 2004; McGrath and Chesler 2004; Hill *et al.* 2009). Mutual understanding between mothers and health professionals was enhanced when mothers felt that their effort and responsibility in caring for their child was recognized (Hodgkinson and Lester 2002).

Reflection point

Think about your clinical placements and a time when you needed to communicate effectively to both parents about their child's condition.

- What approach did you use?
- Was it effective?
- Would you do anything differently next time?

Communicating with parents around the time of diagnosis

The diagnosis of a child with a health condition is a very stressful time for parents (Osborne and Reed 2008; Sanjari *et al.* 2009) and parents retain vivid memories about health professionals' behaviour at this crucial time (Kelleher 2002; Davies *et al.* 2003; Ygge and Arntez 2004; Nuutila and Salanterä 2006). Parents of injured children are often initially distraught, as the most precious thing in their lives has been hurt and they frequently express feelings of guilt (Hopia *et al.* 2005). Parents want a preliminary diagnosis with clear instructions about how to deal with the situation. Parents also need guidance and support to enable them to offer support to their child (Ygge and Arntez 2004). The way in which you relate and work with parents at the time of diagnosis is paramount and can set the tone for your future relationship (Davies *et al.* 2003; Howells and Lopez 2008). Professional scepticism before a child's diagnosis is affirmed can cause some parents to feel resentful and lose confidence and trust in the healthcare team (Swallow and Jacoby 2001). When seeking clarification of information, some parents have reported being dismissed, patronized, ignored or palmed off (Koshti-Richman 2008).

A key aspect is the extent to which the child is acknowledged and spoken to – and about – in a personal and humane manner (Carter *et al.* 2002; Cone 2007). Parents have mixed emotions – on the one hand, there may be relief at a diagnosis (Hodgkinson and Lester 2002; Ygge and Arntez 2004), while on the other, the permanent nature and the implications associated with the diagnosis can generate feelings of deep or chronic sorrow (Clubb 1991; May 1996; Mallow and Bechtel

1999). Hummelinck and Pollock (2006) reported that parents often reached 'information overload' at the time of diagnosis, particularly when a diagnosis required multidisciplinary input and secondary management care for the condition. Parents want information about possible diagnoses and clarity about their options in the delivery of care to their child (Ygge and Arnetz 2004). However, some parents felt that there was insufficient information given for conditions, such as asthma, that were managed in primary care settings (Hummelinck and Pollock 2006). This highlights the need to address the individual needs of all parents. Factors such as educational levels and cultural needs are important variables that need to be considered (Sanjari *et al.* 2009). Shin and White-Traut (2005) reported that nurses frequently sought and gave suggestions, opinions, and information when communicating with parents. Nurses need to recognize the retrospective information needs of parents and predict and create opportunistic times to provide this information, in a format that the parents can assimilate without unnecessarily increasing their anxiety (Hummelinck and Pollock 2006; Sanjari *et al.* 2009).

Activity

What are your perceptions of parental involvement in healthcare settings? Discuss with your colleagues.

Good communication can be improved when conducted in an environment conductive to enabling parents and health professionals to articulate information and questions in more depth and reduce the need of parents to 'parent in public' (Cone 2007: 34). Parents also need opportunities to hear critical information or receive educational sessions separate from their child. This enables parents to express their fears and concerns away from their child. Parents value honesty and frankness in their communication with professionals and believe this helps them to build trust in the healthcare team (Swallow and Jacoby 2001). A positive environment also reduces the risk of parents hearing information not pertinent to their child's care, causing them to misinterpret direct or indirect comments and gestures as significant (Orzalesi and Aite 2011). Healthcare professionals need to show that they are listening to parents, as without such signals parents will stop talking (Howells and Lopez 2008).

The use of medical jargon or medical equipment is not always a barrier to communicating with parents. Nicholl (2007) relates how she used the word 'fit' when talking to a mother about the management of her child's seizures and was reproached by her for not using the term 'seizure'. Swallow and Jacoby (2001) reported how X-ray films coupled with clearly drawn diagrams were used by one medical care team to explain children's diagnoses, which reassured mothers about their children's future care under that healthcare team. Communicating with parents from a psychosocial perspective should not detract from the need to relate to biomedical subject matters (Langewitz *et al.* 2010), as parents require hard facts to make important decisions.

The ongoing relationship between healthcare professionals and parents

The relationship between parents and health professionals will change over time. Over a prolonged period, many parents feel that they are able to manage their child's care, and develop strategies and flexible ways of integrating the daily care of their child into family life (Sloper 2000; Mazurek Melnyk and Fishbeck Feinstein 2001; Dellve *et al.* 2006; Nuutila and Salanterä 2006). Parents' sense of expertise develops around their child's care and skilful negotiation with health professionals about issues concerning the care can result in the development of expert decision-making on the part of parents (Swallow and Jacoby 2001; Carter *et al.* 2002).

Families with a child with a long-term illness share many of the same concerns in their day-to-day lives. Carter *et al.* (2002) suggest there is a need to conceptualize parents' experiences as a process during which their needs for support and information change. Two-way dialogue between families and health professionals is an important prerequisite to building relationships based on mutual trust (Carter *et al.* 2002). Heller and Solomon (2005) reported that a good relationship between health professionals and caregivers was most likely when a personal relationship had been established between them, and the child was seen as an individual in that context. Carter *et al.* (2002: 451) also acknowledged the importance of 'knowing the child' and saw this relationship as the 'most important thing' for parents. A positive relationship between parents and health professionals was shown to assist parents in developing considerable expertise in caring for their child, as they became more experienced in interacting with health professionals and were willing to assume and assert their role (Kirk 2001). Consequently, the varying needs of individual parents need to be acknowledged.

Activity

Ygge (2007) suggests that younger and less experienced nurses may experience difficulties separating their role as a nurse and being friendly with parents who are of similar age. Consequently, parents may feel that serious concerns should be addressed to a more senior nurse.

- What do you think?
- How do you act towards parents?
- Discuss with a colleague.

Communication strategies to enhance the relationship between parents and health professionals

Nurses take the role of communicator with parents in healthcare settings (Ygge 2007) and are viewed as especially important in interpreting information, aiding understanding of treatment, and promoting compliance for parents (Hodgkinson and Lester 2002). The continuity of nursing staff in healthcare settings also provides stability of care for parents, which is not possible within medical teams due to training rotations (Hodgkinson and Lester 2002). Nurses, including students, have better opportunities to develop therapeutic relationships with parents, especially in areas like paediatric oncology (Hawes 2005). It is very important that you are clear about the information that you are seeking from parents and to establish what parents already know. It is necessary to recognize when parents are tired and possibly less receptive to giving or receiving information. Face-to-face communication using a 'lay person's style and language' (Swallow and Jacoby 2001: 760) inspires confidence in parents, especially in cases where nurses can explain the diagnosis in a way that parents understand (Nuutila and Salanterä 2006; Sanjari *et al* 2009). All terminology needs to be explained when talking with parents to ensure clarity and mutual understanding. Constructive advice can be offered to parents in the form of problem-solving as new issues arise (Ball *et al.* 2012).

The level of participation by parents in their child's care should be established when the child is to undergo a painful procedure (Ygge 2007). It is very important to relay information and be prepared to repeat this often so reinforcing understanding. Good communication is a two-way process – it is important to remember that parents know their child best and that their knowledge should be utilized. A balance between closed and open (descriptive, exploration of feelings) questions is effective in most situations when communicating with parents. Closed questions (e.g. Does your child have pain?) are useful for obtaining specific information when parents are distressed or anxious. Open, purposeful questions (e.g. Can you tell me about your child?) are valuable in exploring parental concerns and allowing parents to give different perspectives on their feelings and understanding of a given situation. The appropriate use of responses such as 'yes', 'that's true', and 'hmm-hmm' helps the flow of conversation and encourages parents to continue the dialogue. Facilitative responses using gestures such as nodding, leaning forward, and maintaining eye contact demonstrate that the professional is really listening while verbalizing encouraging phrases such as *huh* words. Effective communication skills require healthcare professionals to be active listeners, to give their full attention to the parent and allow them to speak without interruption, while concentrating on understanding the message (Kacperek 1997; Smettem 1999; Apker *et al.* 2006). You will need to be cognisant of how parents' interpretation of information can be misconstrued. Sudia-Robinson and Freeman (2000: 145) report parents in their study inferring from comments by health professionals, such as 'take a break from the bedside' and 'get some rest', as implying that they were 'in the way'.

Good communication can take time. In the process of listening, you can learn valuable information about parents and their families' situation and home environment (Hopia *et al.* 2005). It is vital not to prejudge the child and family based on what is documented about them (Koshti-Richman 2008). Rules and expectations between parents and health professionals need to be clarified to reduce inconsistencies in care (Fisher and Broome 2011). Reading from or writing notes should be kept to a minimum when engaging with parents. It is important to explain why certain information is recorded and to ensure that what has been said is summarized to ensure understanding. This demonstrates to the parent that you have been listening to them and helps you to organize their thoughts and change the direction of the communication if warranted (Howells and Lopez 2008). Remember also, parents may have different or additional needs since you last spoke to them. By asking about any new concerns directly, communication can be improved and last minute 'by the way's' avoided (Howells and Lopez 2008). It is possible to reinforce positive communication by being sensitive to the words and actions of the parents and their child (Swallow and Macfayden 2004), and where appropriate health professionals can draw from their personal experiences when analysing the situation. Non-verbal cues can be important – such as appropriate eye contact without staring (Apker *et al.* 2006; Ygge 2007; Sanjari *et al.* 2009).

Reflection point

- How good are you at active listening?
- Do you think you are considered to be a good listener by others, including parents?

Activity

Consider the following and discuss with your colleagues:

- How does a poor listener behave in a conversation?
- How do you know when someone is not listening?

Language and cultural barriers in communicating with parents

Effective communication between health professionals and parents in what may not be the parents' first language can be challenging. Time and economic constraints can hinder the relationship between parents and the healthcare team with less than adequate reciprocal information being provided (Wales *et al.* 2008). A professional interpreter may be warranted, requiring coordination of multidisciplinary teams to focus on essential information through a designated health professional. It is also important to be aware of the cultural needs of parents without stereotyping, as each family will have its own views around many issues. Providing time for parents to answer probing questions around their beliefs can assist in providing culturally competent care (Cone 2007). This can assist in gaining an understanding of the various cultural approaches to the 'sick role' and not presupposing parents' reactions (Smettem 1999).

Activity

Review patient information literature used in your healthcare setting that is language- and culture-specific.

Written communication

Communication skills include good record-keeping and are essential for all health professionals to ensure continuity of care (Koshti-Richman 2008). Ygge and Arnetz (2004) suggest a written checklist regarding information about routines in health-care settings, schedules concerning the child's care, and expectations about the parents' role as a means of facilitating communication between the family and healthcare providers (Moore and Kordick 2006). As health professionals, one of your aims is to educate parents, so it is important to elicit how they learn best – by reading or hearing the information, or by visual display (Cone 2007).

Conclusion

This chapter has examined ways in which you can improve communication with parents of children with healthcare needs from the perspective of family centred care. Recognizing the different needs of mothers and fathers as parents of the sick child is important. Communication at the point of diagnosis is critical. It is important to adopt strategies to support communication as a vital part of the therapeutic relationship between parents and health professionals.

Key messages

- Effective communication requires a collaborative relationship between parents and health professionals while recognizing that parents know their child best.
- Parents need information to be repeated, reinforced, and responded to in a manner that allows them to feel that they have been heard.
- Information should be consistent from all health professionals and information that is important to parents should be discussed.

References

Allen, S.M. and Hawkins, A.J. (1999) Maternal gatekeeping: mother's beliefs and behaviours that inhibit greater father involvement in family work, *Journal of Marriage and the Family*, 61(1): 199–212.

Ammentorp, J., Kofoed, P.E. and Laulund, L.W. (2010) Impact of communication skills training on parents' perceptions of care: intervention study, *Journal of Advanced Nursing*, 67(2): 394–400.

Apker, J., Propp, K.M., Zaba Ford, W.S. and Hofmeister, N. (2006) Collaboration, credibility, compassion, and coordination: professional nurse communication skill sets in health care team interactions, *Journal of Professional Nursing*, 22(3): 180–9.

Ball, J.W., Bindler, R.C. and Cowen, K. (2012) *Pediatric Nursing: Caring for Children*. Upper Saddle River, NJ: Pearson Education.

Board, R. (2004) Father stress during a child's critical care hospitalisation, *Journal of Pediatric Health Care*, 18(5): 245–9.

Cannon, E., Schoppe-Sullivan, S.J., Mangelsdorf, S.C., Brown G.L. and Szewcyk Sokolowski, M.S. (2008) Parent characteristics as antecedents of maternal gatekeeping and fathering behaviour, *Family Process*, 47(4): 501–19.

Carter, B., McArthur, E. and Cunliffe, M. (2002) Dealing with uncertainty: parental assessment of pain in their children with profound special needs, *Journal of Advanced Nursing*, 38(5): 449–57.

Central Health Services Council (1959) *The Report of the Committee on the Welfare of Children in Hospital (The Platt Report)*. London: HMSO.

Chesler, M. and Parry, M. (2001) Gender roles and/or styles in crisis: an integrative analysis of the experiences of fathers of children with cancer, *Qualitative Health Research*, 11(3): 363–84.

Clubb, R.L. (1991) Chronic sorrow: adaption patterns of parents with chronically ill children, *Paediatric Nursing*, 17(5): 461–6.

Cone, S. (2007) The impact of communication and the neonatal intensive care environment on parent involvement, *Newborn and Infant Reviews*, 7(1): 33–8.

Corlett, J. and Twycross, A. (2006) Negotiation of parental roles within family-centred care: a review of the research, *Journal of Clinical Nursing*, 15(10): 1308–16.

Coyne, I. (2008) Disruption of parent participation: nurses' strategies to manage parents on children's wards, *Journal of Clinical Nursing*, 17(23): 3150–8.

Davies, R., Davis, B. and Sibert, J. (2003) Parents' stories of sensitive and insensitive care by paediatricians in the time leading up to and including diagnostic disclosure of a life-limiting condition in their child, *Child: Care, Health and Development*, 20(1): 77–82.

Dellve, L., Samuelsson, L., Tallborn, A., Fasth, A. and Hallberg, L.R.M. (2006) Stress and well-being among parents of children with rare diseases: a prospective intervention study, *Journal of Advanced Nursing*, 53(4): 392–402.

Department of Health and Children (2009) *Palliative Care of Children with Life-Limiting Conditions in Ireland – A National Policy*. Dublin: Department of Health and Children.

Devault, A., Milcent, M.P., Quellet, F., Laurin, I., Jauron, M. and Lacharité, C. (2008) Life stories of young fathers in contexts of vulnerability, *Fathering*, 6(3): 226–48.

Fägerskiöld, A. (2006) Support of father's infants by the child health nurse, *Scandinavian Journal of Caring Sciences*, 20(1): 79–85.

Fisher, M.J. and Broome, M.E. (2011) Parent–provider communication during hospitalization, *Journal of Pediatric Nursing*, 26(1): 58–69.

Goldberg, W.A., Tan, E.T. and Thorsen, K.L. (2009) Trends in academic attention to fathers 1930–2006, *Fathering*, 7(2): 159–79.

Griffin, T. (2006) Family-centred care in the NICU, *Journal of Perinatal and Neonatal Nursing*, 20(1): 98–102.

Hawes, R. (2005) Therapeutic relationships with children and families, *Paediatric Nursing*, 17(6): 15–18.

Hawthorne, K., Bennert, K., Lowes, L., Channor, S., Robling, M. and Gregory, J.W. (2011) The experiences of children and their parents in paediatric diabetic services should inform the development of communication skills for healthcare staff (the DEPICTED study team), *Diabetic Medicine*, 28(9): 1103–8.

Heller, K.S. and Solomon, M.Z. (2005) Continuity of care and caring: what matters to parents of children with life-threatening conditions, *Journal of Pediatric Nursing*, 20(5): 335–46.

Hill, K., Higgins, A., Dempster, M. and McCarthy, A. (2009) Fathers' views and understanding of their roles in families with a child with acute lymphoblastic leukaemia: an interpretative phenomenological analysis, *Journal of Health Psychology*, 14(8): 1268–80.

Hodgkinson, R. and Lester, H. (2002) Stresses and coping strategies of mothers living with a child with cystic fibrosis: implications for nursing professionals, *Journal of Advanced Nursing*, 39(4): 377–83.

Hopia, H., Paavilainen, E. and Åstedt-Kurki, P. (2004) Promoting health for families of children with chronic conditions, *Journal of Advanced Nursing*, 48(6): 575–83.

Hopia, H., Tomlinson, P.S., Paavilainen, E. and Åstedt-Kurki, P. (2005) Child in hospital: family experiences and expectations of how nurses can promote family health, *Journal of Advanced Nursing*, 14(2): 212–22.

Howells, R. and Lopez, T. (2008) Better communication with children and parents, *Paediatrics and Child Health*, 18(8): 381–5.

Hummelinck, A. and Pollock, K. (2006) Parents' information needs about the treatment of their chronically ill child: a qualitative study, *Patient Education and Counselling*, 62(1): 228–34.

Kacperek, L. (1997) Non-verbal communication: the importance of listening, *British Journal of Nursing*, 6(5): 275–9.

Kelleher, D. (2002) The lived experience of fathers of chronically ill children: a phenomenological study, Unpublished MSc thesis, University of Manchester.

Kirk, S. (2001) Negotiating lay and professional roles in the care of children with complex health care needs, *Journal of Advanced Nursing*, 34(5): 593–602.

Koshti-Richman, A. (2008) Listening to parents and carers of children with disabilities, *Paediatric Nursing*, 20(7): 43–4.

Kowalski, W., Leef, K.H., Mackley, A., Spear, M.L. and Paul, D.A. (2006) Communicating with parents of premature infants: who is the informant?, *Journal of Perinatology*, 26(1): 44–8.

Langewitz, W., Heydrich, L., Nübling, M., Szirt, L., Heidemarie, W. and Grossman, P. (2010) Swiss Cancer League communication skills training programme for oncology nurses: an evaluation, *Journal of Advanced Nursing*, 66(10): 2266–77.

Mallow, G.E. and Bechtel, G.A. (1999) Chronic sorrow: the experience of parents with children who are developmentally disabled, *Journal of Psychosocial Nursing*, 7(7): 31–5.

May, J. (1996) Fathers: the forgotten parent, *Pediatric Nursing*, 22(3): 243–6, 271.

Melnyk, B.M. and Feinstein, N.F. (2001) Coping in parents of children who are chronically ill: strategies for assessment and intervention, *Pediatric Nursing*, 27(6): 548–58.

McGrath, P. and Chesler, M. (2004) Fathers' perspectives on the treatment for pediatric hematology: extending the findings, *Issues in Comprehensive Pediatric Nursing*, 27(1): 39–61.

Moore, J.B. and Kordick, M.F. (2006) Sources of conflict between families and healthcare professionals, *Journal of Pediatric Oncology Nursing*, 23(2): 82–91.

Mu, P., Ma, F., Hwang, B. and Chao, Y. (2002) Families of children with cancer: the impact on anxiety experienced by fathers, *Cancer Nursing*, 25(1): 66–73.

Nicholl, H. (2007) Involving mothers in research studies: practical considerations, *Paediatric Nursing*, 19(1): 28–30.

Nuutila, L. and Salanterä, S. (2006) Children with a long-term illness: parent experiences of care, *Journal of Pediatric Nursing*, 21(2): 153–60.

Orzalesi, M. and Aite, L. (2011) Communication with parents in neonatal intensive care, *Journal of Maternal-Fetal and Neonatal Medicine*, 24(1): 135–7.

Osborne, L.A. and Reed, P. (2008) Parents' perceptions of communication with professionals during the diagnosis of autism, *Austism*, 12(3): 309–24.

Pleck, J.H. and Hofferth, S.L. (2008) Mother involvement as an influence on father involvement with early adolescents, *Fathering*, 6(3): 267–86.

Sanjari, M., Shirazi, F., Heidari, S., Salemi, S., Rahmani, M. and Shoghi, M. (2009) Nursing support for parents of hospitalised children, *Issues in Comprehensive Pediatric Nursing*, 32(3): 120–30.

Shin, H. and White-Traut, R. (2005) Nurse–child interaction on an inpatient paediatric unit, *Journal of Advanced Nursing*, 52(1): 56–62.

Simmerman, S. and Blacher, J. (2001) Fathers' and mothers' perceptions of father involvement in families with young children with a disability, *Journal of Intellectual and Developmental Disability*, 26(4): 325–38.

Sloper, P. (2000) Predictors of distress in parents of children with cancer: a prospective study, *Journal of Pediatric Psychology*, 25(2): 79–91.

Smettem, S. (1999) Welcome/Assalaam-u-alaikaam: improving communications with ethnic minority families, *Paediatric Nursing*, 11(2): 33–5.

Sudia-Robinson, T.M. and Freeman, S.B. (2000) Communication patterns and decision making among parents and healthcare providers in the neonatal intensive care unit: a case study, *Heart and Lung*, 29(2): 143–8.

Swallow, V.M. and Jacoby, A. (2001) Mothers' evolving relationship with doctors and nurses during the chronic illness trajectory, *Journal of Advanced Nursing*, 36(6): 755–64.

Swallow, V. and Macfayden, A. (2004) Nurses' communication skills: are they effective research tools?, *Paediatric Nursing*, 16(5): 20–3.

Tiedje, L.B. and Darling-Fisher, C. (2003) Father-friendly healthcare, *American Journal of Maternal Child Nursing*, 28(6): 350–7.

Troilo, J. and Coleman, M. (2004) College student perceptions of the content of father stereotypes, *Journal of Marriage and Family*, 70(1): 218–27.

Wales, S., Crip, J., Moran, P., Perrin, M. and Scott, E. (2008) Assessing communication between health professionals, children and families, *Journal of Children and Young People's Nursing*, 2(2): 77–83.

Ygge, B.M. (2007) Nurses' perceptions of parental involvement in hospital care, *Paediatric Nursing*, 19(5): 38–40.

Ygge, B.M. and Arnetz, J.E. (2004) A study of parental involvement in pediatric hospital care: implications for clinical practice, *Journal of Pediatric Nursing*, 19(3): 217–23.

6 Communicating with siblings of children with healthcare needs

Colman Noctor and Emer Murphy

This chapter will examine the interpersonal effect childhood illness has on children who have a brother or sister who requires medical treatment. It is a mistake to presume that it is only during hospital admissions that siblings are negatively affected by the loss of parental attention; rather, 'parental availability' is the currency to measure possible disruption to siblings' lives in all circumstances. This lack of parental availability can be equally as disruptive, for example, in the case of caring for a sibling at home as much as while in hospital, as in some cases this is experienced as even more distressing due to the intrusion this has on normal family life at home. Indeed, sometimes the enduring nature of some illnesses can mean that the longevity of intervention can lead to a sense of hopelessness and a feeling that things will never change for the siblings involved. This chapter will use the phrase 'treatment journey' to describe interventions that include both periods of hospitalization and ongoing care needs that can occur on an out-patient basis or indeed in the family home. We use the case example of Tim and Lisa (brother and sister) to illustrate the experiences of a family during a child's illness.

Learning outcomes

By the end of this chapter you should be able to:

1. Describe the dynamical processes that can occur for families during times of crisis and identify how healthcare professionals can bring forward the needs of siblings to their parents' attention in an appropriate and effective way
2. Outline ways in which normal family functioning can be maintained through difficult times and reflect on ways to limit the negative impact of childhood illness on a functioning family system
3. Appreciate how healthcare professionals can keep the family in mind while treating a young person and their family within their particular setting

Introduction

When a young person becomes unwell and requires medical treatment, there is a surge of understandable activity around that youngster. Both parents can become consumed by the quest to improve the young patient's wellbeing and alleviate their suffering. In these circumstances, there is often another individual (or group of individuals) who inadvertently suffer as a result of this illness. These are the young patient's siblings. During the course of a brother or sister's illness, siblings can feel left out and can suffer loneliness, anger, resentment, and guilt. Without any ill intention by their already overburdened parents, siblings are often inadvertently ignored during this time, which can have a significant effect on their psychological wellbeing and happiness (Spinetta et al. 1999).

Alderfer et al. (2010) suggest that siblings of children with serious illness are an at-risk group psychosocially and should be provided with appropriate support services. They go further and suggest that siblings can experience a significant subset of experiences such as post-traumatic stress symptoms, negative emotional reactions (e.g. shock, fear, worry, sadness, helplessness, anger, and guilt), and poor quality of life in emotional, family, and social domains. Alderfer et al. suggest that, in general, distress is greatest close to the time of diagnosis and school difficulties are also evident within two years of diagnosis. Massie (2010) also recommends that there is a clear need for sibling psychosocial interventions. It is therefore vital that we as health professionals broaden our awareness beyond the nominated patient and consider the impact on the family system and the young siblings.

Communication difficulties of families during the illness of a child

In a seminal text, Spinetta et al. (1999) configured a set of useful guidelines and principles that apply to the care of siblings throughout the treatment process and divided them into three discrete categories. We will refer to the work of Spinetta et al. (1999) throughout, as their findings remain relevant today.

The first category: isolation

Throughout the treatment journey, from the point of diagnosis, siblings can feel isolated or abandoned. This can be a real or imaginary abandonment and both are equally as disturbing to the sibling in question. In the case of the acute phases of childhood illness, parents frequently spend long periods in the hospital and are therefore away from the family home. This can result in siblings being cared for by extended family members or family friends and this can evoke a sense of feeling unwanted or of being a burden. Often, this is also compounded by the fact that when parents eventually collect the well sibling from the temporary carers, they are tired and preoccupied and lack the energy or resolve to attend to the needs of the well sibling (Spinetta et al. 1999).

Vignette   Young siblings' experience of isolation

Tom is a 13-year-old boy who is suffering from leukaemia. Tom has been in and out of hospital for the last two years. Tom has one sister Lisa who is 12 years old. Over the last two months, Tom has been receiving intensive treatment in hospital and he is responding well. His parents have been taking it in turns staying with him each night. His sister Lisa stays with various extended family members and friends most nights, as it is often late at night when one parent returns home and then has to leave early the following morning to relieve the other parent to go to work. Lisa hates not being at home but she feels she cannot say this to her parents as she notices that they are already so stressed. Lisa has been known to cry herself to sleep at night, a fact that no one is aware of.

Reflection point

- How do you imagine Lisa feels in this scenario?
- Is this situation a result of understandable parental preoccupation or a child protection issue?
- What is the role for you as a nurse in helping Lisa?

The second category: tolerating the unknown

It is a normal human reaction to respond in an anxious way to uncertainty. Even much of adult anxiety is perpetuated by a fear or anticipation of the unknown or the unexpected. It is a common belief that children 'do not need to know the details' of events that are deemed 'too difficult to understand', and therefore parents sometimes choose to keep siblings in the dark about the condition and treatment of their ill brother or sister. This is a well-intended attempt to 'protect' the sibling from the scary and unnecessary details that come with the truth (Spinetta et al. 1999).

In our work in the mental health field, we are often responsible for taking a full family history of stressful events or traumas that have occurred in families. Often during this process we are struck by parents' inaccurate estimation about their children's awareness of familial stressful events. It is often the case that during the recording of a family history, parents may recall a stressful event and inform us that it was 'kept from' their child so that they 'would not be affected' by it. However, most mental health professionals are never surprised by the revelation that the child, who is often interviewed separately, has an uncannily accurate recollection of the event and though not informed directly has displayed the ability to pick up on and interpret the atmospheric stress and therefore come to a conclusion of their own. Furthermore, in many cases the imagined or estimated scenario concocted by the young person can be more distressing than had he or she been appropriately informed about the true event at the time.

It is important to remember that some children become more receptive when they are anxious. Anxious children can develop a sort of emotional antenna that can pick up on the slightest expressions of parental anxiety or fear. This is understood as a survival mechanism that encourages the young person to be extra sensitive to changes in their environment due to a pervading fear of being kept in the dark about something important. A young sibling can become more clingy or demanding of parental attention when they perceive it to be in short supply. The young sibling can become inordinately demanding and may choose to express this when their parent is engaged, for example, in a brief conversation with a friend. This is often reflected in the young sibling pulling on their parent's arm or sweater in order to draw their attention away from the conversation with their friend and towards something else. This is usually something very innocuous that the child has just noticed but feels it necessary to point out immediately. This is a classic example of an insecure young sibling trying to remind their parent of their presence and importance.

Vignette   Keeping siblings in the dark

Lisa has not visited her brother in the last two weeks. Despite wanting to, her parents have said she needs to take a break from going to the hospital as it is 'too much for her'. Lisa is suspicious that there are other reasons for her parents not wishing her to visit. Last night she overheard her aunt (with whom she is staying) on the phone to her neighbour. Her aunt mentioned on the phone that 'things were bad' and that Lisa's dad 'will be in an early grave if he keeps going the way he is going'. When Lisa inquired how things were, she was informed that 'everything is fine'. Lisa is now worried that both her brother and her dad will die and she cannot get any straight answers from anyone.

Reflection point

- What would help Lisa in this situation?
- Is her aunt to blame for Lisa's distress?
- How would any young child interpret the throwaway remark that Lisa's aunt used on the phone?

There is a point to protecting young siblings from medical information that they may not understand, and we are at pains to indicate that a full description of the sick child's illness is neither necessary nor helpful to young siblings. However, an acknowledgement and appropriate explanation of what is happening should help to manage the sibling's anxiety, and later in the chapter we describe ways in which this information can be communicated.

The third category: developmental considerations in communication

All communication with young people should take into account their particular life stage and developmental level. Childhood and adolescence are periods of dramatic change throughout which the young person's capacity for understanding alters greatly (Spinetta *et al.* 1999). The six-year gap between a 10-year-old and a 16-year-old young person exemplifies the growth spurts that occur physically, socially, and emotionally. This developmental gap narrows with age, so that the same six-year gap represents a far less maturational difference between, say, a 40-year-old and a 46-year-old adult. It is with this in mind that all interventions with young people be pitched at an age-appropriate level. The different trajectories of development are also important. These trajectories can vary from young person to young person and even differ within the same young person. This can be seen in the 12-year-old who has developed a quite sophisticated intellectual capacity but displays immaturity in the areas of social and emotional development. It is because of these processes that health professionals need to carefully consider these different capacities and tailor their interventions accordingly. Health professionals need also to be aware of the developmental regression that can occur in young siblings who feel abandoned or vulnerable.

The concept of communication with young siblings

For most young siblings, the responsibility for eliciting information from and about their ill brother or sister lies with their parents and health professionals (Gowers 2001). Overall, the process of communication is quite complex (Seden 2007), as it requires a commitment from professionals to gain an understanding of, and appreciation for, the relationship each young sibling has with him/herself, family, friends, peers, community, school, learning, and leisure (Cobb and Counihan 2009). Multiple tools and frameworks have been suggested as a means of effecting such communication. Many communication strategies adopt an investigative and questioning approach to information gathering that when applied to children and adolescents proves unsuccessful. When communicating with young siblings, we recommend creating the context for a supportive, non-confrontational style of communication (Morrison-Valfre 2005), which is a more suitable and constructive technique when attempting to engage young people who may be in some way distressed.

Most young people who have siblings with a serious illness may have trouble voicing their worries (Chelser and Alsweade 1991). Often, open communication can prove difficult when attempting to fully realize a young sibling's level of distress, as young people in general tend to communicate more through behaviour than words (Garbarino and Stott 1992). Thus, a comprehensive approach to communication provides the ideal arrangement, as it affords health professionals and parents an opportunity to observe young siblings' reaction and interaction to changes in their social, emotional, environmental, familial, and psychological states. Subsequently, it provides valuable information regarding the range of personal skills, responses, and trauma held by each sibling, which can later be used to assist health professionals in refining their ongoing formulation of their difficulties (Varcarolis *et al.* 2006). It is likely that there are certain common characteristics of all young people who have a sibling with a serious illness, including a general inability to recognize or express their feelings or needs. This is similar to Rosner's (2003) view about young people's modes of communicating. Given that these are the typical attributes of the sibling of a seriously ill young person, due diligence must be employed to ensure such issues are adequately addressed when formulating a philosophy of response (Morrison-Valfre 2005).

Steps to effective communication with siblings in hospital

The following subsections are based on five elements of successful treatment highlighted by Gunderson (see Pratt *et al.* 2007: 175): containment, structure, support, involvement, and validation.

Containment

A fundamental concept in managing anxiety is psychological 'containment'. This involves ensuring that both the physical and psychological wellbeing of the young sibling is addressed (Varcarolis *et al.* 2006). This means taking the necessary steps to ensure that the young sibling feels free from threat. Through the use of therapeutic containment, the young sibling ought to experience an environment that encourages open and honest communication, the free expression of feelings and that which reassures them of their parents' ability to cope with and manage the various difficulties their sick sibling is going through together with any anxieties they might have. Containment is necessary to provide safety and to foster trust (Stuart 2009). An example of containment could include reassuring the young sibling that they did not cause their brother or sister's illness and it is not their responsibility to make them better. It is also important that the sibling of the sick child has a relationship with someone (ideally outside of the immediate family) who they trust and from whom they can receive objective reassurance about their worries. In terms of how containment aids the process of communication, the creation of a 'safe place' cannot be overestimated. Young siblings often find it difficult to trust adults and as a result may be unwilling to reveal details of their inner thoughts and fears unless they are sure that to do so may be of benefit to them. The existence of a contained environment communicates to young siblings that their parents are willing to impose necessary external controls to keep them and their environment safe (Stuart 2009). As a result, they can become more comfortable/confident in expressing their thoughts or fears in relation to their sibling's illness. It is important that health professionals assess the network of support for siblings and, where appropriate, offer time for them to discuss their fears and provide a containing relationship where they can receive honest and age-appropriate information as well as someone to hear their worries.

Vignette   Addressing siblings' worries

Tom's treatment team hear that he has a sister who is one year younger than him and inquire from his parents how she is coping. When the family describe the current arrangement for Lisa (i.e. that Lisa is staying with extended family most nights), the team suggest that some provisions be put in place to support Lisa to have time with one or both of her parents. The family agree that they will ask dad's sister, who is normally charged with looking after Lisa, to do a shift in hospital with Tom instead. During this time Lisa and her parents can go to the cinema and have something to eat. Lisa's parents are encouraged to discuss with Lisa how she is coping with all of the disruption to normal family life and invite her to ask questions. Lisa has developed a strong relationship with her older cousin Vikki who is 17. Dad picks up on this relationship and has asked Vikki to check in with Lisa at regular intervals and allow her to discuss her worries about mum, dad, and Tom. This creates a possibility to contain Lisa's worries and offers her a window of support.

Reflection point

- Do we all need containing relationships in our lives?
- Who do you go to for emotional containment?
- Why is Vikki an important person for Lisa in this scenario?

Structure

Structure refers to all aspects of daily life that encourage the predictable organization of time, place, and person (Stuart 2009). Dependability in activity and the environment not only reduces young people's level of anxiety but also increases their feelings of safety (Delaney 1991). A predictable structure provides order in times of chaos. This is particularly important within the context of the hospitalization of a young person, where a lot of unpredictability can increase adverse behavioural, emotional or cognitive patterns in siblings (Varcarolis *et al.* 2006). Additionally, routine and predictability create an air of calm throughout family systems, which can also be beneficial. Having a notional idea of visiting times, childminding arrangements, and the facilitation of other normal activities is important when introducing the concept of structure (Elder *et al.* 2008). Therefore, it is important to set aside protected time for parents to spend with the healthy child, organize it so that parents take it in turn to visit the sick child so that at least one parent can be at home with the healthy sibling, plan in advance who will collect the sibling from school, and allow time for the young sibling to verbalize their concerns or worries.

Such structure informs communication and aids the identification of a variety of ways to counteract the maladaptive effects of dysfunction, chaos, and unpredictability. Although these are common features when a family is trying to adjust to coping with a child that has a serious illness, the institution of structure will help to minimize their effects. Malone *et al.* (1997) were aware of this fact when they suggested that placing young people in general in a structured environment alone was enough to evoke an improvement in presentation generally and mental health status specifically. Thus, a young sibling's response and reaction to a structured environment can provide much useful information when devising communication strategies during a period of childhood illness.

Vignette   Siblings' need for predictable structure

Lisa is beginning to display some clingy behaviours that are out of character. Just yesterday her mother was due to collect her from her aunt's at 7 pm and they were going to spend the night together at home. Unfortunately, her mum was delayed leaving the hospital and did not collect Lisa until 8.30. Lisa normally has to go to bed at 9.30 and therefore knew that her time at home would be limited. When her mum arrived to pick her up, Lisa's aunt offered her mum a cup of tea as she looked tired. Lisa's mum accepted. Lisa knew this would be a further delay and she began to moan and sigh. Mum scolded Lisa for her demonstrative behaviour and asked her to have 'a bit of consideration'. Lisa just wanted to be at home and now she felt extremely guilty for upsetting her mum.

Lisa's mum needs to be reminded of the importance of structure for Lisa, and that this seemingly irrelevant delay in picking her up is the reason for her disgruntlement and perhaps mum's blasé approach upon arrival did not help to validate Lisa's need for predictable structure.

Reflection point

- Why is Lisa so upset that her mum is having a well-deserved cup of tea?
- Is Lisa being inconsiderate?
- How come Lisa's mum cannot see how important every minute is at home for Lisa?

Support

Support includes parents' conscious efforts to help the young sibling feel better and to gain a greater understanding of their emotional needs (Rawlins *et al.* 1993). Support relates to the unconditional acceptance of a young sibling regardless of circumstances (Stuart 2009). The goal of support is to calm the young sibling, to help them to feel safe, and to promote a sense of hope and wellbeing. Support is often focused on the young person who is unwell and therefore there may be a corresponding lack of support for the well sibling. Spinetta *et al.* (1999) highlight the merit of keeping hope alive when communicating with the siblings of sick children, suggesting that it is of the uppermost importance. Support can be communicated by being emotionally available to the young sibling, offering encouragement and reassurance when they visit their brother or sister in hospital, explaining what they can expect to see when they enter their brother/sister's room, and interacting in a respectful way (Elder *et al.* 2008).

The situations that occur as a result of taking care of a seriously ill child at home are generally new and ambiguous to both the young patient and the family unit as a whole (Reinecke *et al.* 2003). Consequently, the help and understanding required are quite significant. A supportive focus ensures that such assistance is given, while also providing parents with an opportunity to gain information about the young sibling's interpretation of events. Similarly, reassuring interactions with parents can empower young siblings to adapt better to the challenges they face – an issue which can later be capitalized on when identifying ways in which the young sibling can become involved or included in the process of caring for their sick brother or sister. Furthermore, supportive conversations can help parents to clarify how much a young sibling understands about health and illness, something that is worthy of exploration given the circumstances.

Vignette   Supportive conversation and inclusion

Lisa has made a picture frame for Tom so that he can have a collection of family photos in his room in hospital. Lisa needs some special glue to finish off her picture. On the way home from the hospital she asks if they can stop to buy this and both parents who are exhausted state they have not got time and will do it tomorrow. Lisa is forlorn but does not make a fuss. Later that evening dad notices Lisa trying to struggle to finish her frame using tape. Dad realizes her efforts and says that he will take her to buy the glue now. Lisa and dad go to the shop to buy the glue and dad asks Lisa if she is worried about Tom. Lisa says she is very worried as she feels Tom may never come home. Dad reassures Lisa that Tom will come home and asks her if she would like to be involved in helping him paint Tom's room for his return. Lisa is delighted with this plan and thinks about what colours Tom would like.

Here dad picks up on Lisa's need for support and reassures her that Tom will be home. Dad's idea of painting the room helps them both to focus on a positive outcome.

Reflection point

- Why might Lisa feel it is important for Tom to have pictures of his family in his hospital room?
- What might Lisa be unconsciously communicating to her parents as she assumes that Tom might be missing his family?
- How important is dad's recognition of Lisa's need for support and what message does his plan to decorate Tom's room convey to the worried Lisa?

Involvement

No amount of communication or dialogue can be considered constructive if the young sibling is not actively engaged as a partner in the process. As Noctor (2008) correctly highlights, one cannot claim to understand completely what the needs of young people are without discussing this with them first. Involvement means getting the young sibling as engaged as possible in the functions of caring for the sick child, including them in all appropriate decision-making and allowing them to become actively involved both practically and emotionally (Rawlins *et al.* 1993). Such involvement should be at a level that the young sibling is comfortable with and at which they do not feel over-burdened.

Again from a communication viewpoint, involvement can prove very useful. By involving the young sibling in family activities and practices, parents are promoting the idea that the young sibling is a vital part of the family unit who has equally valid contributions and suggestions to make. Involvement also encourages the young sibling to take ownership and responsibility for their own behaviour. How they subsequently interpret and handle such concepts can help to determine and shape what issues they may need more support or encouragement with in the future.

Vignette   Siblings' involvement

Lisa is in the hospital one day when the nurse is tending to Tom's physical needs. Tom and Lisa are playing the X-Box when the nurse arrives. When the nurse is checking Tom over, she notices that Lisa is no longer attending to the game but is looking intently at what the nurse is doing. The nurse asks her if she knows what the various beeping machines mean. Lisa says she does not. Tom looks surprised. The nurse suggests that Tom might explain these 'beeping contraptions' to Lisa. Tom then gives Lisa a wonderfully clear explanation of each machine's function. The nurse is impressed and commends Tom's knowledge and comments that perhaps Lisa might be able to help Tom with these various checks once he is back home. Lisa laughs and returns to the X-Box game far less worried.

Validation

Validation requires that the individuality, values, and beliefs of the young sibling are recognized. It is the act of affirming their world-view (Stuart 2009). Actively listening, acknowledging the feelings underlying their personal experience, and attempting to understand the meaning behind behaviour, all reinforce the young sibling's sense of individuality and serve to validate their experience. Since each of us is unique and different in terms of how we interpret and respond to life's challenges, the process of engagement and communication must also be different from person to person. Validation can be conveyed through respecting the rights, opinions, and decisions of the young sibling. Examples of validation include respecting the young sibling's wish to visit or not to visit their brother/sister while in hospital, recognizing how difficult things are in the family as a result of having a sick child, acknowledging the positive efforts being made by all the family members, and reminding the young sibling that they are just as important as their sick brother or sister.

The significance and benefit of validating how a person feels and what they have experienced is well documented in the literature (Keltner *et al.* 2007). Nowhere is this need more apparent than within the context of a family unit with a sick child. The simple act of validating the young sibling's experience of events can itself be cathartic and pave the way for future interactions between parent and child that are of a more sincere quality (Norman and Ryrie 2009), thus making communication a more rich and meaningful experience.

Vignette   Validating siblings' experience

Lisa's parents find out that there is a group for siblings being held in the hospital and they suggest Lisa attends. When she goes to the first group, most of the children there are far younger then she is. When she returns she says that she felt uncomfortable and does not want to go again. Her dad feels that she should go anyway but mum picks up on her discomfort and decides that these groups are not for everyone and suggests that she only needs to go if she wants to.

Reflection point

- Should Lisa be made to attend this group, as it is the only support available in the hospital?
- How might Lisa feel while she is in the playgroup with the younger children?
- Is mum or dad right in their response to Lisa?
- Who is displaying a validation of her experience?

Conclusion

This chapter has highlighted the need for healthcare teams to be aware of the risks to siblings of children with serious and enduring illness. The chapter began by emphasizing the need to pay close attention to siblings' needs during the care of their ill brother or sister. Psychological interventions with siblings of child patients can effectively reduce psychological maladjustment and improve medical knowledge about the illness (Prchal and Landolt 2009). It is thus crucial that immediate family members and health professionals keep siblings of ill children in mind at all times. It is the duty of those entrusted with the care of a child and their family that they highlight the risks of any healthcare treatment to the whole family. This is a sensitive time for families and one must exercise extreme sensitivity while addressing these issues. It is important that healthcare teams treat the family as a system, where each component has its own value. It is easy to become consumed by the needs of the named patient in care and run the risk of mirroring parents' neglect of siblings' needs. Nurses play a vital role in keeping siblings in mind and directing families to do the same. The communication skills required with young siblings include clarity, support, and reassurance. It is hoped through the examples given in this chapter that you have gained an insight into the needs of young siblings and been made aware of some methods of identifying these needs and responding to them. It is also useful to be aware of any sibling support groups facilitated by your organization. By providing the family and parents with support you assist the young sibling too.

Key messages

- Treating children holistically involves being aware of the impact of the illness on the whole family. Many times we are drawn to the needs of the ill child and their parents. It is vital to consider the effects on siblings also.
- We may believe that because something is not discussed openly in front of children they remain blissfully unaware of the facts. In reality, children are able to pick up on stresses in the family unit and form their own conclusion.
- Remember that anxiety is a fear of the unknown. Therefore, appropriate information can assist in reducing anxiety as opposed to adding to it. Everyone must have the right to ask a question and have it answered, especially in a situation of potential stress and significant anxiety.

References

Alderfer, M.A., Long, K., Lown, E., Marsland, A., Ostrowski, N., Hock, J. *et al.* (2010) Psychosocial adjustment of siblings of children with cancer: a systematic review, *Psycho-Oncology*, 19(8): 789–805.

Chelser, M.A. and Alsweade, J. (1991) Voices from the margin of the family: siblings of children with cancer, *Journal of Psychosocial Oncology*, 9: 19–42.

Cobb, J. and Counihan, S. (2009) *Assessment and Therapeutic Interventions in Child and Adolescent Mental Health.* Galway: National University of Ireland.

Delaney, K. (1991) Nursing in psychiatric milieus part 2: mapping conceptual footholds, *Journal of Child and Adolescent Psychiatric Nursing,* 5(1): 15–17.

Elder, R., Evans, K. and Nizette, D. (2008) *Psychiatric and Mental Health Nursing.* Sydney, NSW: Mosby Elsevier.

Garbarino, J. and Stott, M. (1992) *What Children Can Tell Us: Eliciting, Interpreting and Evaluating Critical Information from Children.* San Francisco, CA: Jossey-Bass.

Gowers, S.G. (2001) *Adolescent Psychiatry in Clinical Practice.* London: Arnold.

Keltner, N., Schwecke, L. and Bostrom, C. (2007) *Psychiatric Nursing,* 5th edn. St. Louis, MO: Mosby.

Malone, R., Luebbert, J., Delaney, M., Biesecker, K., Blaney, B., Rowan, A. *et al.* (1997) Nonpharmacological response in hospitalized children with conduct disorder, *Journal of the American Academy of Child and Adolescent Psychiatry,* 36: 242–7.

Massie, K. (2010) Frequency and predictors of sibling psychological and somatic difficulties following pediatric cancer diagnosis, DPhil thesis, University of Toronto.

Morrison-Valfre, M. (2005) *Foundations of Mental Health Care,* 3rd edn. St. Louis, MO: Mosby.

Noctor, C. (2008) *Therapeutic considerations in child and adolescent mental health units,* unpublished paper disseminated at meeting in University College Dublin, 8 August.

Norman, I. and Ryrie, I. (2009) *The Art and Science of Mental Health Nursing,* 2nd edn. Maidenhead: Open University Press.

Pratt, C.W., Gill, K.J., Barrett, N.M. and Roberts, M.M. (2007) *Psychiatric Rehabilitation,* 2nd edn. New York: Elsevier Academic Press.

Prchal, A. and Landolt, M.A. (2009) Psychological interventions with siblings of paediatric cancer patients: a systematic review, *Psycho-Oncology,* 18(12): 1241–51.

Rawlins, R., Williams, S. and Beck, C. (1993) *Mental Health – Psychiatric Nursing: A Holistic Life-cycle Approach.* London: Mosby-Year Book.

Reinecke, M., Dattilio, F. and Freeman, A. (2003) *Cognitive Therapy with Children and Adolescents: A Casebook for Clinical Practice,* 2nd edn. New York: Guilford Press.

Rosner, R. (2003) *Textbook of Adolescent Psychiatry.* London: Arnold.

Seden, J. (2007) Assessing the needs of children and their families, *Research and Practice Briefing Paper 15.* Available at: http://www.york.ac.uk/depts/spsw/mrc/documents/QPB15.pdf (accessed 11 July 2012).

Spinetta, J.J., Jankovic, M., Eden, T., Green, D., Martins, A.G., Wandzura, C. *et al.* (1999) Guidelines for assistance to siblings of children with cancer: Report of the SIOP Working Committee on Psychosocial Issues in Pediatric Oncology, *Medical Pediatric Oncology,* 33(4): 395–8.

Stuart, G. (2009) *Principles and Practice of Psychiatric Nursing,* 9th edn. St. Louis, MO: Mosby Elsevier.

Varcarolis, E., Carson, V. and Shoemaker, N. (2006) *Foundations of Psychiatric Mental Health Nursing: A Clinical Approach,* 5th edn. St. Louis, MO: Saunders Elsevier.

7 Communicating with children and their families during sensitive and challenging times

Philip Larkin

The theme of this chapter is communicating with children and families during the sensitive and challenging times of life-limiting illness, death, and dying. Three key questions are addressed: How can I prepare a parent for the impending death of a child? How can I prepare a child for the impending death of a parent? How can I communicate appropriately with a child who is dying? The chapter will focus on two critical areas: communication around diagnosis and prognosis, and caring communications with children and families up to and including death and dying.

Learning outcomes

By the end of this chapter you should be able to:

1. Articulate the value of a family centred care approach to developing appropriate communication strategies in life-limiting illness
2. Understand better ways of communicating effectively with children and families in the context of life-limiting illness, particularly in the breaking of bad news
3. Appreciate the relationship between cognitive development and children's interpretation of death

---

Introduction

A useful starting point is to reflect on the meaning behind the story of Cecilia in *Through the Glass, Darkly* (Gaarder 1999). In this book, which narrates the conversations between a dying child and her guardian angel, Ariel, the reader is exposed to the way in which communication unfolds in a very particular way at times of pain and sadness; the suffering of a mother who cannot bear the impending loss of her daughter, the wisdom of a grandmother who understands the natural cycle of living and dying, a younger sibling who lives for the here and now and for whom death is not part of his understanding. In the final conversation between Cecilia and Ariel, they are sitting on the window-ledge, looking down on her body in the bed. Cecilia remarks that she looks beautiful in sleep. Ariel replies she is more beautiful now that she is released from her body and the sickness that she experienced. Cecilia replies 'But I can't see that for myself, because now I am on the other side of the looking-glass' (Gaarder 1999: 161). The key premise of this book is that we often view the world of communicating around death with children and their families as if through dark glass. We cannot see things absolutely clearly because we are human, and some things are so profound that we can only see them when we begin to finally understand why they are important and meaningful to us. The impact of life-limiting illness in children can be a little like this. When children are healthy and vibrant, we assume that it will always continue to be so. The child will move through adolescence to adulthood with many aspirations, hopes, and dreams. For some, however, this is not the case, and the child's journey becomes one of health to ill-health, debilitation and, in some cases, death. In others, the fact that life expectancy is limited can be evident from birth or, as in Josh's case, from the consequences of chronic illness. This demands specific skills on the part of health professionals, not least the ability to support the child and family through devastating and traumatic events.

Vignette   Limited life expectancy from birth: Josh's story

Josh, a 6-month-old boy with a congenital heart defect, was admitted to the unit with respiratory distress. He became increasingly unwell during this admission and the team decided that further medical intervention was inappropriate. Through a family meeting, the changing goals of care were explained to the family and the need to focus on extended comfort measures clarified. Though distressing for both parents and staff, the decisions taken led to Josh being able to spend his last 48 hours at home, supported by community care services and with his extended family.

Activity

Consider the following questions and make some notes to support your learning:

- What would be important for Josh's parents to know when the goals of care changed?
- How should the professional carers prepare for meeting Josh's parents to tell them the decision about his future care planning?
- What do you think Josh's parents and other relatives need most if Josh is going to be taken home for his final days of life?

Death in childhood

Of the 1.5 billion children in the world, 11 million die before the age of 5. Of these deaths, half are related to the effects of malnutrition (Field and Behrman 2003). In Western societies, the death of a child is something perceived as unnatural and unwarranted. Data show that up to 50,000 children die in the USA each year (birth to adolescence), of whom 70 per cent have genetic and/or congenital disease (e.g. cystic fibrosis, mucopolysaccharidosis). Cancer is responsible for a somewhat smaller number of childhood deaths (Field and Behrman 2003). A recent review of palliative care services for children in the UK (Craft and Killen 2007) was unable to establish numbers of children with life-limiting illness but did indicate an expected increase, as children live longer due to advancing technological supports. In Ireland, the Department of Health and Children (2009) indicated there are approximately 1600 children living with a life-limiting condition, of whom 66 per cent are likely to die and the majority of such childhood deaths (71 per cent) occur in the first year of life; in effect, there are approximately 350 childhood deaths per year from life-limiting conditions. Looking at all the data, it is clear that death in childhood is rare in Western society and thus health professionals often lack the requisite skills to address death and dying because the number of cases is relatively small.

Interpreting trajectories of life-limiting illness in children

Hynson *et al.* (2006) present a trajectory of transitions for a child with life-limiting illness. The child may die because:

- their treatment for a potentially curative illness failed;
- he or she has a condition from which premature death may be expected even with intensive treatment;
- there is no cure for the condition;
- the child is at risk of early death due to the complications associated with chronic disability or non-progressive disease.

Caring for children at end-of-life is challenging because the prognosis of many conditions is hard to predict and often requires multiple complex interventions across a limited lifespan. Compared with adult-oriented constructs of palliative and end-of-life care (WHO 2002), these trajectories demonstrate that there is rarely a clear point at which treatment and care goals shift to paediatric palliative care alone, and definitions of life-limiting illness and end-of-life care do not necessarily imply impending death (Hynson *et al.* 2006). Whereas most adult-oriented palliative care services tend to focus on cancer (with some notable exceptions), less than half of all children who die do so from a malignant condition (Jones *et al.* 2002). This means a complicated and multi-faceted communication approach is frequently needed. This is reflected in the commonly accepted definition of palliative care for children:

Palliative care is an active and total approach to care, embracing physical, emotional, social and spiritual elements. It focuses on enhancement of quality of life for the child and support for the family and includes the management of distressing symptoms, provision of respite, and care following death and bereavement.

(ACT/RCPCH 1997)

It is clear that any communication strategy needs to focus on child and family as one unit, addressing needs during life, through the dying phase, and into the bereavement period. Four categories of life-limiting illness for children have been proposed (see Box 7.1). Note that Together for Short Lives has produced a useful set of definitions in relation to palliative care for children, which are available at http://www.act.org.uk.

Box 7.1 Categories of life-limiting illness (ACT/RCPCH 1997)

1. Life-threatening conditions for which curative treatment may be feasible but can fail (e.g. cancer)
2. Conditions where premature death is inevitable and where there may be long periods of intensive treatments aimed at prolonging life and allowing participation in normal activities (e.g. cystic fibrosis)
3. Progressive conditions without curative treatment options, where treatment is exclusively palliative and may extend over years (e.g. Batten disease, mucopolysaccharidosis)
4. Irreversible but non-progressive conditions causing severe disability, leading to susceptibility to health complications and likelihood of premature death (e.g. cerebral palsy)

Each of the categories in Box 7.1 exhibits a different pathway of illness and dying. For example, a child and family who receive a cancer diagnosis may focus initially on cure using active treatments such as chemotherapy. They will regularly seek to discuss progress (sometimes called *upstream palliative care*). If cure is not possible, they may achieve a significant period of remission, followed by relapse, further ineffective treatment, and eventually death (Field and Behrman 2003). Compare this with the trajectory of a chronic life-limiting disease such as cystic fibrosis, where the child may become seriously ill but be offered emergency interventions (such as intravenous antibiotics) on a number of occasions until the symptom burden becomes so great that recovery is not possible and death occurs (Field and Behrman 2003). In other cases, such as neurodegenerative disease, a stepwise progression to death with a relatively slow deterioration over years is common. Given the fact that each of these trajectories is unique, effective communication needs to address the child, family, wider networks of support, and the community as an intrinsic whole.

Family-oriented end-of-life care

The ideal of partnership resonates with the view that best practice in family-oriented end-of-life care is defined by the strength of relationship. A compassionate response to the experiences of children and families is a first step in developing this relationship (Svavarsdottir 2006). The way in which health professionals address family needs impacts on parents' interpretation of such experience (Bohn *et al.* 2003; Limacher and Wright 2003; Duhamel and Talbot 2004). Exploring family needs requires the practitioner to be willing to engage in the narrative that has shaped the family's health and illness experience in a way that neither alienates nor contradicts their interpretation of that experience (Chesla 2005). Communication is a reflective process and working with children and families in times of stress requires practitioners to question how this experience of family caring either aligns with or differs from their own personal experience of family. Practitioners need to access a resource to share those reflections, as many practitioners – and nurses in particular – fail to express the emotional burden of care (McCloskey and Taggart 2010). In the following sections, a theoretical case study is used to focus the discussion, followed by a brief reflection on how theory can be translated and articulated in practice. The first case considers the needs of life-limiting illness at birth, the second care in the context of a dying parent, and finally, and perhaps most challenging, working with a dying child.

Communication around diagnosis and prognosis

Vignette   Life-limiting illness diagnosed at birth: Anthony's story

After a series of miscarriages, Anthony was Claire and Tom's first baby. Claire had an uneventful pregnancy and delivery with no notable complications during labour. At birth, the midwife immediately noted that Anthony seemed to be very 'floppy' and he was taken away to the paediatric intensive care unit. Claire and Tom were told that Anthony was being monitored overnight because he was 'unwell' and needed to be observed. Next morning, a doctor met Claire and Tom and explained that Anthony showed some physical and neurological characteristics resonant with Patau syndrome (Trisomy 13). She explained to Claire and Tom that Anthony's condition was 'not conducive with life' and he was unlikely to survive beyond the first week of life.

Activity

Consider the following questions and make some notes to support your learning:

- What feelings might you expect Claire and Tom to have in relation to the news about Anthony?
- What questions may they have in the coming days for the healthcare team?
- How would you respond?

A starting point for supporting Clare and Tom is to be conscious of how the news will impact on their self-perception as parents. Having sought parenthood, the fact that their newborn child will not survive will dash any hopes for a future as a family together. Feelings of hopelessness, devastation, anger, and distress associated with a grief response would be expected. An equally important factor to consider is how Tom and Claire function as a couple. Kissane and Bloch (2002) identify three typologies of family function that can determine how well people can cope with loss and move towards some degree of resolution: *cohesiveness* (how well they can be together in their grief), *adaptiveness* (including resolution of conflicts), and *expressiveness* (the showing of emotion to one another). These coping strategies may only become evident over time, and for the physician delivering the bad news about Anthony, it may be difficult to make any prediction.

Cues in communication strategies

Health professionals often fail to pick up 'cues' that are offered in clinical situations either consciously or unconsciously (Heaven *et al.* 2006). Strategies often seen in practice include the use of jargon in explanations, failing to be attentive to what is being said, blocking (or seeming to ignore a point made), and offering premature reassurance (Heaven and Green 2009). Cue-based communication has become a gold standard in the education of healthcare professionals (Clayton *et al.* 2009). Cues may be verbal or non-verbal, including using words or phrases that express immediate shock and disbelief, failing to make eye contact, and indeed silence (Del Piccolo *et al.* 2006). Failure to acknowledge the first cue will determine subsequent interactions.

Breaking bad news

The telling of truth in a sensitive manner is essential. In Anthony's case, clear messages need to be delivered about the life-limiting nature of his disease with some reference to prognosis where possible. Language needs to be respectful of the parents' capacity to understand. It may be more appropriate to say 'It is not likely that Anthony will live very long because of his illness' rather than 'Anthony's illness is not conducive to life', which may not convey the reality of the situation to Tom and Claire. Practical questions may need to be addressed, such as referral to support agencies in the community if discharge is a possibility. If death is likely to occur soon, as is common in Patau syndrome, and home discharge is not possible, it is important that Tom and Claire understand this so that they can make decisions regarding care planning, such as staying with Anthony if they wish and coming to terms with the need to consider funeral arrangements.

At some point, Tom and Claire will need to consider whether to undergo genetic counselling on future pregnancies, and thus their sense of loss may equally reflect the loss of future children as well as that of Anthony (Knebel and Hudgings 2002; Read 2002). Because parents may have had no idea of a genetic problem until their child is born, they may experience guilt at passing on the genetic abnormality. Although probably not the case for Tom and Claire, since the diagnosis of Patau syndrome is likely to rule out future pregnancies, discussions may be required with wider family members and with other children who may themselves have the disease. Parents may be facing the loss of multiple children (Knebel and Hudgings 2002; Price *et al.* 2005).

Caring communications with the child and family up to and including death

Vignette   Care in the context of a dying parent: Mary's story

Mary was a 39-year-old woman, a mother of two children, Alice aged 9 and Jason aged 3. She was diagnosed with breast cancer and despite a full range of active cancer treatment, her disease rapidly advanced and it became apparent that she might die in the near future. Both Mary and her husband Andrew, although aware of her imminent death, were unsure how to approach the issue with their children.

Activity

Consider the following questions and make some notes to support your learning:

- What do you think Mary's greatest fears are as she approaches the end of her life?
- What concerns would you have for Alice and Jason in understanding what is happening to their mother?
- What advice could you offer Mary and Andrew in addressing their children's questions at this time?

Children may face long-lasting psychological and emotional distress from the trauma associated with the death of a close adult, especially a parent (Schuurman

2003; Kirwin and Hamrin 2005). Addressing the 'pre-death' needs of a child by their parent can impact significantly on the overall outcome for the child's experience, and the earlier the intervention, the better for the child (Kirwin and Hamrin 2005; Kraus 2005). Stone *et al.* (1999) offer a useful model to understand how difficult conversations work and with which a child-oriented framework for communication can be applied. The person who is communicating the information needs to understand how and why it is perceived in a particular way and what meaning is given and taken by the information shared. Given the complexity of understanding in explaining concepts such as death and dying, clarity is crucial. In an adult-oriented world, bad news is often interpreted relative to people's feelings of safety and security, the need for control, the need to feel recognized and to belong (Back and Arnold 2003). For children, these basic human needs may be all the more evident and demonstrated through a range of emotions, including distress, anger, frustration, fear, and/or regressive behaviours. Therefore, Alice and Jason's responses to the news may be unpredictable.

The importance of child development in death communication

The child development theories of Jean Piaget (1896–1980) have been applied to the context of death, dying, and grief. Although there has been critique of Piaget's research methods, the findings have resonance with experience, albeit with the caveat that progression may not be clearly attributable to age. An understanding of the cognitive stages of child development assists in understanding the child's interpretation of abstract concepts associated with death and dying, such as irreversibility, finality, inevitability, and causality (Schum and Kane 2009). For infants, for example, loss of attachment to a parent or home due to prolonged hospitalization on the part of the parent may inhibit infant bonding. A younger child may consider illness as punishment for something they did. Older children may rebel against authority and refuse to attend school, and adolescents may be at risk of social isolation, loneliness, and depression at a time when external relationships beyond the family unit are important for social development (Farrelly 2009). Given the spectrum of possible responses from children, being able to appreciate their stage of cognitive development can assist in planning a communication strategy (Table 7.1).

Approaches to communication

Jason and Alice's ability to understand that their mother's life is now of limited duration is dependent on how they perceive the world and to what extent they understand illness and death. It is essential to frame the sharing of information in developmentally appropriate language, yet retain the clarity of the message (Schum and Kane 2009). Early intervention is essential and Mary and Andrew, supported by other family members, should raise the issue with the children as soon as they feel able. Whether or not this involves healthcare professionals should be determined by the parents, as it may be that Mary and Andrew seek professional advice but wish to address the issue themselves. Advice, where given, needs to focus on developmental capacity to understand and interpret the situation and practical

Table 7.1 Stages of cognition (derived from Piaget)

Name	Age	Stage	Understanding and interpretation	Approach
Jason	3	Pre-operational	Fears loss of control and being left alone. May see death as a temporary state. Perceives stress in carers	Needs stability and routine. Begin process as early as possible, using pictures, stories, and make-believe play. Physical contact with Mary and Andrew
Alice	9	Concrete operational	Death may be a fear in itself. Fears disappointing others. Developing mature understanding of death	Maintain structure and routine. Encourage questions and social contacts outside the home. Allow child to participate in decision-making, where possible. Encourage diversion (trips away, DVDs). Provide reassurance

advice on how to begin and end the conversation. It is important not to withhold information, as children do have the capacity to understand, relative to their development, and they should be afforded every opportunity to participate fully in the process of approaching death and preparing for a funeral (Christ 2000; Chowns 2005). Finding ways to reduce isolation, provide a forum for expression of feelings, and diminish intense levels of emotion can assist with the normal structure and routine that children need (Saldinger *et al.* 2004; Stokes 2004). Given the age difference and likely difference in response, it may be that Jason and Alice would be told separately. Alternatively, they could be told together and then followed up separately. For Jason, the fact that he may perceive the stress in others may indicate foresight and planning in how and what is to be said and by whom. Alice may have innumerable questions that need to be answered and where information is required, this should be given (Brown and Warr 2007). An important point for Alice is that there should be no sense of 'putting on a brave face for Jason' or 'being a big girl'. Since fear of disappointing others may be an issue for her, this may lead to a disconnection with her own feelings so as not to upset others.

Creative support strategies

A wide range of children's books are available that address issues of living and dying. Deciding which to use may be based on some of the following questions related to the family system:

- Does the family have a religious belief or belief in an afterlife?
- Are the family more comfortable with nature and life-cycle stories?

- Has there been any other experience of death in the family (grandparent, pet)?
- What is the attention span of the child? Do they like reading?
- Is the message clear from the book (e.g. sadness and crying is normal behaviour)?
- Can the child either read or look at the pictures independently?

It is possible to find a range of books to meet these needs, as well as specialized workbooks that involve activities and creative arts for the expression of feelings. Creative exploration may include the creation of a memory 'jar' or box (Richies and Dawson 2000), where mementos, photographs, and letters are stored and over time used as a way of remembering Mary and, most importantly, the children's relationship with her. With advancing technology, this may include the use of home-made DVDs and podcasts. Pre-bereavement support groups may be of benefit to some children (Kennedy *et al.* 2008; Popplestone-Helm and Helm 2009). Models proposed suggest that bringing the child and well carer into a group setting may facilitate communication, build relationships, and empower families to make choices (Popplestone-Helm and Helm 2009).

A child's response to dying

Vignette   Caring for a dying child: Peter's story

Peter was an 11-year-old boy with a history of Duchenne muscular dystrophy (DMD). His decline was progressive and advanced more quickly than expected. Following considerable breathing difficulties, a decision was taken to provide supportive ventilation in the paediatric intensive care unit (PICU). When Peter did not improve, a further decision was taken to undertake compassionate extubation, which took place in his home, with his parents and stepsister present. Peter died peacefully, supported by his local paediatric hospice team and PICU staff from the hospital. His funeral was a celebration of his life attended by the whole community as well as those who had cared for him professionally.

Activity

Consider the following questions and make some notes to support your learning:

- What concerns you most about caring for a dying child?
- What would most help Peter's parents and sister in their home during his last days?
- What advice might you offer Peter's parents on planning his funeral?

Children who are dying can experience significant psychological distress as they face the reality of impending death (Brown and Warr 2007; Schum and Kane 2009; Wright *et al.* 2009). The fear that children experience can relate to physical, psychological, and/or social elements related to their illness; fear of pain, loss of function, distress at saying goodbye and about being forgotten. Given the intensity of relationship between a parent and child, it is important to consider what this means in terms of life losses – of self, of future, and of dreams (Rosenblatt 2000). Beale *et al.* (2005) offer a strategy for addressing children's need to communicate with others about their illness and death. There should be early agreement to speak openly and honestly between all family members and caregivers, including the dying child. Information should be developmentally appropriate, discussed at an appropriate time with the child, explorative of how much information is sought, and offer realistic reassurance about the dying process in an empathetic and caring manner. The integrity of the family structure should be maintained. Peter's life-limiting condition and its concomitant outcomes may have given him a maturity and wisdom beyond his years. He may reflect on the implications of his illness in relation to the possibility of death and realize its impact on his future (Schum and Kane 2009). This would naturally influence the way in which communication with Peter was managed.

Social networking

Given Peter's age and the fact that he will have developed a social network through school and play, it is important to create a clear communication network to advise the wider community of progress, in addition to immediate family members. This is as much to assist them to prepare school friends and others for the fact that Peter is dying and to develop ways of expressing their sadness, contribute to the funeral if asked (for example, a guard of honour or to provide music) and, if appropriate, to visit the house or funeral home after death.

At the time of death

Retaining the structure of the family unit in the immediate period before, at the time of, and shortly after death is important. Parents need time to say goodbye to their child, and allowing time to hold and stay with their child's body is important (Meyer *et al.* 2002; Davies 2005). Events that take place at the time of death will remain in family members' memory and so attention needs to be paid to how procedures and practices are carried out that respect the values and wishes of the family (Komaromy 2004). Normalization of the situation is important. Deciding on what clothes the dead child will wear, items to be placed in the coffin, and decisions on roles and responsibilities at the funeral (Richies and Dawson 2000; Davies 2005; DeJong-Berg and Kane 2006), all give a sense of control at a time when everything appears uncontrollable. Foster and Gilmer (2008) argue that grief is not about severing ties with the person who has died, but reintegrating them into the family structure in a different way. In time, the importance of anniversaries, visits to the cemetery or crematorium and remembrance at birthdays will become an important part of this integration process.

Family members

Seminal research by Bluebond-Langner (1978) identified that siblings of children with life-limiting illness are exposed to chronic sorrow. Brown (2002) explored the specific needs of siblings of children cared for in one UK children's hospice, although it is acknowledged that there is generally a lack of evidence about effective interventions with this group. Inclusiveness is a priority to help avoid alienating children who may feel angry, hurt, and confused about what is happening. Some children may blame themselves for the situation (perhaps over a small incident that happened with their dying sibling). They may be jealous of the dying child because of the attention he or she is receiving, then feel guilt about that jealousy, given the situation.

Adolescence is a particularly complex time for adjustment to grief and loss. Oscillation between the need to adopt adult approaches to feelings of loss and the need to be supported and comforted by the parent can lead to frustration and 'acting out' (i.e. staying out late, drinking, antisocial behaviour). Siblings can experience intense frustration at not being able to live a 'normal' life. There may be greater expectations in terms of contributions at home. It may be more difficult to develop a social life outside the home or bring friends home. They may become overly protective of their sibling and disengage from social activity. Most challenging of all is where the sibling may have the same genetic disease as their dying brother or sister. A number of voluntary and statutory agencies may be involved in providing support, for example, Barnardos and Winston's Wish. These agencies may be able to provide a network to allow grief to be managed therapeutically in a safe and secure environment.

There is limited understanding of how grandparents perceive the death of a grandchild, although there is some suggestion that they may experience a 'double-grief' reaction – for their own adult child as well as the grandchild (Reed 2000; Brown and Warr 2007). Grandparents can be hugely supportive in maintaining the normality of routine in a family, creating space for the parents to manage the complex needs of their dying child. They may have had their own personal experience of grief and loss and indeed of a child themselves, which may be both helpful to share and painful to recall. They may have had an intensely personal relationship with their sick grandchild that they did not have with their own child, and so some sense of the family dynamic and inter-generational relationship should be understood by the healthcare professional. Grandparents may hold a pivotal role in the family dynamic and this may be more overt in some cultures. It is important that their needs are incorporated into care planning and their presence valued at the time of the death of their grandchild.

Conclusion

The international development of children's palliative care services has the potential to address the challenges of managing the needs of children with a life-limiting illness, not least by developing partnership models for transitional care and seeing parents and families as core to that partnership (Brown and Warr 2007).

Communication in this complex area of care begins with a response to the family as a unit, respecting their values and beliefs and being cognisant of how these reflect those of the professional carer. Learning the skill of being present for children and their families in the midst of their suffering (Schum and Kane 2009), and being able to instil a sense of cohesion to the way care is managed, can bring comfort and hope for a peaceful resolution at a difficult and often traumatic time.

Key messages

- Caring for a child with a life-limiting illness should, as far as possible, focus on the family as the primary source of communication, information-giving, and emotional support.
- Children interpret and understand death and dying in a very different way to adults.
- An understanding of the child's cognitive development will assist in the planning of supportive care to both child and family in the context of life-limiting illness.

References

Association for Children with Life-threatening or Terminal Conditions and Their Families and Royal College of Paediatrics and Child Health (ACT/RCPCH) (1997) *Definition of Paediatric Palliative Care*. Available at: http://www.act.org.uk (accessed 11 July 2012).

Back, A.L. and Arnold, R.M. (2003) Dealing with conflict in caring for the seriously ill, *Journal of the American Medical Association*, 293: 1374–81.

Beale, E.A., Baile, W.F. and Aaron, J. (2005) Silence is not golden: communicating with children dying from cancer, *Journal of Clinical Oncology*, 23: 3629–31.

Bluebond-Langner, M. (1978) *The Private Worlds of Dying Children*. Princeton, NJ: Princeton University Press.

Bohn, U., Wright, L.M. and Moules, N.J. (2003) A family systems nursing interview following a myocardial infarction: the power of commendations, *Journal of Family Nursing*, 9(2): 151–65.

Brown, E. (2002) *The Death of a Child*. Birmingham: Acorns Children's Hospice Trust.

Brown, E. and Warr, B. (2007) *Supporting the Child and Family in Paediatric Palliative Care*. London: Jessica Kingsley.

Chesla, C.A. (2005) Nursing science and chronic illness: articulating suffering and possibility in family life, *Journal of Family Nursing*, 11(4): 371–87.

Chowns, G. (2005) Swampy ground: brief interventions with families before bereavement, in B. Monroe and F. Kraus (eds) *Brief Interventions with Bereaved Children*. Oxford: Oxford University Press.

Christ, G.H. (2000) *Healing Children's Grief: Surviving a Parent's Death from Cancer*. Oxford: Oxford University Press.

Clayton, J.M., Butow, P.N. and Tattersall, M.H.N. (2009) Telling the truth: bad news, in D. Walsh, A.T. Caraceni, R. Fainsinger, K.M. Foley, P. Glare, C. Goh *et al.* (eds) *Palliative Medicine*. Philadelphia, PA: Saunders Elsevier.

Craft, A. and Killen, S. (2007) *Palliative Care Services for Children and Young People in England: An Independent Review for Secretary of State for Health*. London: Department of Health.

Davies, R. (2005) Mothers' stories of loss: their need to be with their dying child and their child's body after death, *Journal of Child Health Care*, 9(4): 288–300.

DeJong-Berg, M. and Kane, L. (2006) Bereavement care for families part 2: evaluation of a paediatric follow-up programme, *International Journal of Palliative Nursing*, 12(10): 484–94.

Del Piccolo, I., Goss, C. and Bergvik, S. (2006) The fourth meeting of the Verona Network on Sequence Analysis: consensus findings on the appropriateness of provider responses to patients cues and concerns, *Patient Education and Counselling*, 61: 473–5.

Department of Health and Children (2009) *Palliative Care for Children with Life-Limiting Conditions in Ireland: A National Policy*, Dublin: Department of Health and Children.

Duhamel, F. and Talbot, L.R. (2004) A constructivist evaluation of family systems nursing interventions with families experiencing cardiovascular and cerebrovascular illness, *Journal of Family Nursing*, 10(1): 12–32.

Farrelly, M. (2009) Families in distress, in D. Walsh, A.T. Caraceni, R. Fainsinger, K.M. Foley, P. Glare, C. Goh *et al.* (eds) *Palliative Medicine*. Philadelphia, PA: Saunders Elsevier.

Field, M.J. and Behrman, R.E. (2003) *When Children Die: Improving Palliative and End-of-life Care for Children and Their Families*, Washington DC: National Academic Press.

Foster, T.L. and Gilmer, M. (2008) Continuing bonds: a human response within paediatric palliative care, *International Journal of Palliative Nursing*, 14(2): 85–91.

Gaarder, J. (1999) *Through a Glass, Darkly*. London: Phoenix.

Heaven, C. and Green, C. (2009) Good communication: patients, families and professionals, in D. Walsh, A.T. Caraceni, R. Fainsinger, K.M. Foley, P. Glare, C. Goh *et al.* (eds) *Palliative Medicine*. Philadelphia, PA: Saunders Elsevier.

Heaven, C., Clegg, J. and Maguire, P. (2006) Transfer of communication skills training from workshop to workplace: the impact of clinical supervision, *Patient Education and Counselling*, 60: 313–25.

Hynson, T.L., Aroni, R., Bauld, C. and Sawyer, S.M. (2006) Key factors affecting dying children and their families, *Journal of Palliative Medicine*, 8(suppl. 1): 70–8.

Jones, R., Trenholme, A., Horsburgh, M. and Riding, A. (2002) The need for paediatric palliative care in New Zealand, *New Zealand Medical Journal*, 115(1163): U198.

Kennedy, C., McIntytre, R., Worth, A. and Hogg, R. (2008) Supporting children and families facing the death of a parent: part 1, *International Journal of Palliative Nursing*, 14(4): 162–8.

Kirwin, K.M. and Hamrin, V. (2005) Decreasing the risk of complicated bereavement and future psychiatric disorders in children, *Journal of Child and Adolescent Psychiatric Nursing*, 18(2): 62–78.

Kissane, D. and Bloch, S. (2002) *Family Focused Grief Therapy: A Model of Family-Centred Care during Palliative Care and Bereavement (Facing Death)*. Philadelphia, PA: Open University Press.

Knebel, A.R. and Hudgings, C. (2002) End-of-life issues in genetic disorders: literature and research directions, *Genetic Medicine*, 4(5): 366–72.

Komaromy, C. (2004) Nursing care at the time of death, in S. Payne, J. Seymour and C. Ingleton (eds) *Palliative Care Nursing: Principles and Evidence for Practice*. Buckingham: Open University Press.

Kraus, F. (2005) The extended warranty, in B. Monroe and F. Kraus (eds) *Brief Interventions with Bereaved Children*. Oxford: Oxford University Press.

Limacher, L. and Wright, L.M. (2003) Commendations: listening to the silent side of a family intervention, *Journal of Family Nursing*, 9(2): 130–50.

McCloskey, S. and Taggart, L. (2010) How much compassion have I left? An exploration of occupational stress among children's palliative care nurses, *International Journal of Palliative Nursing*, 16(5): 233–40.

Meyer, E.C., Burns, J.P., Griffith, J.L. and Truog, R.D. (2002) Parental perspectives on end-of-life care in the pediatric intensive care unit, *Critical Care Medicine*, 30(1): 226–31.

Popplestone-Helm, S.V. and Helm, D.P. (2009) Setting up a support group for children and their well carers who have a significant adult with a life-threatening illness, *International Journal of Palliative Nursing*, 15(5): 214–21.

Price, J., McNeilly, P. and McFarlane, M. (2005) Paediatric palliative care in the UK: past, present and future, *International Journal of Palliative Nursing*, 11(3): 124–6.

Read, C.Y. (2002) Reproductive decisions of parents of children with metabolic disorders, *Clinical Genetics*, 61(4): 268–76.

Reed, M.L. (2000) *Grandparents Cry Twice: Help for Bereaved Grandparents*. New York: Baywood.

Richies, G. and Dawson, P. (2000) *An Intimate Loneliness: Supporting Bereaved Parents and Siblings*. Buckingham: Open University Press.

Rosenblatt, P.C. (2000) *Parent Grief: Narratives of Loss and Relationship*. Philadelphia, PA: Brunner Mazel.

Saldinger, A., Porterfield, K. and Cain, C.C. (2004) Meeting the needs of parentally bereaved children: a framework for child-centred parenting, *Psychiatry*, 67(4): 331–51.

Schum, L.N. and Kane, J.R. (2009) Psychological adaptation of the dying child, in D. Walsh, A.T. Caraceni, R. Fainsinger, K.M. Foley, P. Glare, C. Goh *et al.* (eds) *Palliative Medicine*. Philadelphia, PA: Saunders Elsevier.

Schuurman, D. (2003) *Never the Same: Coming to Terms with the Death of a Parent*. New York: St Martin's Press.

Stokes, J.A. (2004) *Then, Now and Always*. Cheltenham: Winston's Wish.

Stone, D., Patton, B.M. and Heen, S. (1999) *Difficult Conversations: How to Discuss what Matters Most*. New York: Viking Penguin.

Svavarsdottir, E.K. (2006) Listening to the family's voice: Nordic nurses' movement towards family centred care, *Journal of Family Nursing*, 12(4): 346–67.

World Health Organization (WHO) (2002) *Definition of Palliative Care: National Cancer Control Guidelines. Policies and Managerial Guidelines*. Geneva: WHO.

Wright, B., Aldridge, J., Murr, K., Sloper, T., Tomlinson, H. and Miller, M. (2009) Clinical dilemmas in children with life-limiting illnesses: decision-making and the law, *Palliative Medicine*, 23: 238–47.

8 Communicating with vulnerable and disadvantaged children

Janet Wray and Victoria Stewart

The aim of this chapter is to stimulate discussion and challenge concepts of practitioners' communication skills with children and young people determined as being vulnerable or disadvantaged. Some of these may be the subject of legal processes leading to a local authority being responsible for their care and wellbeing. The chapter begins by reviewing what is meant by 'vulnerable' and 'disadvantaged' children and young people; and moves on to assessment, safeguarding children, sharing information, and barriers to communication, before addressing how to develop skills of communication with these groups of children and young people.

Learning outcomes

By the end of this chapter you should be able to:

1. Understand the nature of vulnerability and disadvantage, clarify your own perspectives on these through reflection, and gain a broader appreciation of the complexity of the topic
2. Appreciate the guidance on safeguarding children and the expectations of professionals when sharing sensitive information
3. Describe new skills and strategies to employ in communicating with vulnerable or disadvantaged children and young people

---

Introduction

Subjectivity and personal experience may influence the practitioner's concept of vulnerable children and young people, and this in turn may impact on interactions during an episode of care. It is useful to explore personal understanding and concepts related to the notions of being vulnerable or disadvantaged. Reflective processes are an ideal framework within which to challenge personal understandings, thoughts, and experiences, and through this improve communication skills with this group of children and young people.

The Department of Children and Youth Affairs (2011) has laid out wide-ranging guidance on the promotion of child welfare and the development of safe practices in work with children. Similarly, the report *Working Together to Safeguard Children* (Department for Children Schools and Families 2010) provides comprehensive guidelines for multi-agency professionals to improve outcomes for all children and young people. Based on the five outcomes as laid down within *Every Child Matters* (Department for Education and Skills 2003), the guidance offers detailed definitions and frameworks for clinicians. The guidance states clearly the need for health professionals to be able to communicate effectively with children and young people to ensure comprehensive assessment and needs analysis. It is, therefore, vital that these skills become embedded in day-to-day clinical practice for children's nurses and other professionals.

Defining vulnerability and disadvantage

For practitioners working directly with children and families, vulnerability and disadvantage may be synonymous with child protection frameworks, and without further thought a subjective view may be taken with the inherent danger of accepting common misconceptions and myths. To ensure optimal health outcomes for children and young people, it is important that health and social care professionals remain objective and do not apply traditional or personal expectations.

Reflection point

Spend five minutes considering your personal understanding of what disadvantage and vulnerability might mean for children. Write down five points for each. Take another five minutes to consider how you have drawn these conclusions.

Activity

Use the Internet to access the Social Exclusion Taskforce and Joseph Rowntree Foundation websites. Read and think about their definitions of vulnerability and disadvantage.

How well do your definitions or preconceptions fit with the explanations presented in the work of these agencies?

Perspectives on vulnerability and disadvantage

Although definitions may vary, vulnerability and disadvantage can be linked with specific socio-economic factors. The Social Exclusion Task Force (2007) identified a number of factors:

- unemployment and low income
- poor housing
- poor parental academic attainment
- parental mental or physical health problems
- substance misuse
- domestic violence.

The Department of Children and Youth Affairs (2011: 11) adds to these: children with disabilities, those who are homeless or who are separated from their parents or other family members, and who depend on others for their care and protection. Another source (Ofsted 2008) suggests that any of the following could be vulnerable:

- looked-after children/care leavers
- children in the family justice system
- children and young people who commit offences
- children who are victims of or witnesses to crime
- children with learning difficulties or disabilities
- children and young people in the armed forces
- young carers
- children using health services
- missing children
- asylum-seeking children
- children from minority ethnic groups
- children in secure settings.

Activity

Think of a child or family that you have worked with recently that may have been disadvantaged or vulnerable.

- Were any of the factors identified by the three agencies above present?
- If they were, was anything done to address these, or was the care similar to that for any other family?

Estimates from the Social Exclusion Task Force suggest that approximately 2 per cent of UK families experience significant day-to-day disadvantage. The Healthy Child Programme (Department of Health 2009) places a strong emphasis on early assessment and interventions for families to reduce the impact of disadvantage. The same focused attention is provided by the Irish Department of Children and Youth Affairs through the Early Years Education Policy Unit, offering targeted early years interventions for children who experience disadvantage.

For children's nurses and other practitioners in both community and acute care environments, it is reasonable to anticipate that a significant number of health interventions will be with children and families from disadvantaged backgrounds and communities. These families will access a range of health and social care services, including the private, voluntary, and independent sectors. This means that effective communication attributes underpin holistic assessment and care planning for all children and families across a range of healthcare settings.

Assessment

Children can be vulnerable for many reasons, and, even though this may not be immediately obvious at the assessment stage, practitioners need to revisit assessments and care plans to ensure that children and young people are offered the opportunity to speak about difficult issues. Even if a good relationship has been built up between a professional and a child, other pressures might discourage the child from divulging sensitive information, particularly without being prompted or asked.

An example of this would be domestic violence at home. Children may hear or see violence or abuse and know that it is wrong, but the parents may have discussed it with them in an attempt to cover it up (or told them directly not to talk about this issue outside the family home). Either of these situations can be approached by asking indirect questions, such as 'How are things at home? Do you have your own space? How does everyone get on with each other?' With younger children, drawing pictures or writing letters to people, which may never be sent, can help a child to express their views and opinions. It is important to remember that circumstances can change quickly in family life and children may become vulnerable at different stages of your professional relationship with them.

From a practitioner's point of view, any children who are subject to neglect or abuse are deemed to be vulnerable. It is important to be aware that parental issues (substance misuse or domestic violence) can impact on children's vulnerability. These are also areas in which practitioners find it difficult to work confidently. Even when cases like this are reported and families are worked with as part of a child protection plan, parents can be needy and demanding. Subsequently, the children's needs may be inadvertently subordinated to the adult's needs. This is another area where practitioners need to remain aware and to check repeatedly that assessment is focusing primarily on children's needs, and that this focus directs the plan.

Safeguarding children and sharing information

Children who are vulnerable may require additional professional support to prevent the situation from becoming worse. Guidance for professionals and agencies in this field is provided through safeguarding policy. One of the more troublesome aspects of this for nurses and others is the issue of confidentiality or, more accurately, what must be disclosed and how.

Information gathering and sharing

When working with children and young people, if any needs are identified that are additional to those already subject to planned care, a review will need to be conducted. When the child is also vulnerable, a multi-agency approach is often required. These additional needs may come to light through one or more of the following:

- disclosure by a child/young person;
- disclosure by another professional (adult or children services);
- disclosure by an extended family member;
- disclosure by a parent.

It is a requirement to communicate effectively with other agencies and family members as well as children and young people who are subject to the additional need. This needs to take place as soon as possible when new information is shared with a practitioner. It is as important to gather information from other agencies as it is to share information with them. This can build up a bigger picture of what is really going on with families, clarify the complexity of problems, and allow for an integrated response from individual professionals and agencies.

Fortunately for practitioners, detailed guidance is available on how to share information appropriately and effectively (Department for Children Schools and Families 2008; Health Service Executive 2011) (see Table 8.1). Local guidance will also be available and should already be embedded in practice. As professionals, understanding information sharing means that nurses can be clear when communicating intended actions to children, young people, and families. If a child is at risk of harm, information sharing becomes an urgent duty of care.

Table 8.1 Information sharing: guidance for practitioners and managers

Remember that the Data Protection Act is not a barrier to sharing information but provides a framework to ensure that personal information about living persons is shared appropriately.

Be open and honest with the person (and/or their family where appropriate) from the outset about why, what, how and with whom information will, or could be shared, and seek their agreement, unless it is unsafe or inappropriate to do so.

Seek advice if you are in any doubt, without disclosing the identity of the person where possible.

Share with consent where appropriate and, where possible, respect the wishes of those who do not consent to share confidential information. You may still share information without consent if, in your judgement, that lack of consent can be overridden in the public interest.

Consider safety and well-being: Base your information sharing decisions on considerations of the safety and well-being of the person and others who may be affected by their actions.

Necessary, proportionate, relevant, accurate, timely and secure: Ensure that the information you share is necessary for the purpose for which you are sharing it, is shared only with those people who need to have it, is accurate and up to date, is shared in a timely fashion, and is shared securely.

Keep a record of your decision and the reasons for it – whether it is to share information or not. If you decide to share, then record what you have shared, with whom and for what purpose.

Source: Department for Children Schools and Families (2008:11)

On the whole, confidentiality means keeping private any details about an individual or about what they have disclosed in discussion or in writing. For children's nurses, key documents provide frameworks and boundaries for the scope of confidentiality and communication with children and young people in clinical practice. The Nursing and Midwifery Council (NMC 2008) states clearly that people have a right to confidentiality. An Bord Altranais (2000) demands a similar standard. Practitioners must, however, disclose information if there is the possibility that someone is at risk of harm. Other professions are guided by similar documentation.

In clinical practice, the consent of the child or young person should be sought prior to sharing any information with other practitioners. This may, however, be superseded by child protection procedures if it is deemed that the child or young person is at risk of harm. The age and competence of the child or young person should be considered in relation to consent. In certain situations, it may be necessary to seek consent from the parent or guardian. This can be a particular challenge to the practitioner if the parent or carer is the source of potential harm. In such circumstances, safeguarding teams in health and social care agencies can offer further advice to the practitioner. Local policies are available to provide additional direction.

It is useful for the practitioner to be equipped with knowledge of the most up-to-date guidance regarding information sharing. Should a child or young person request that a practitioner maintain confidentiality about a potential disclosure, the practitioner has a professional responsibility to advise that dependent upon the nature of the disclosure, it may be necessary to discuss and seek advice from other agencies and professionals.

As with all health interventions, the need for accurate, contemporaneous record-keeping is paramount for the practitioner. Local record-keeping and child protection guidelines should be used to ensure that record-keeping and documentation meet the requirements of local and national governance frameworks.

Barriers to communication

An awareness of the reasons why children and families may have difficulty communicating with professionals is essential. These barriers cause anxiety and stress, and often prevent families engaging effectively with professionals.

Activity

Think about possible barriers to communication when children are vulnerable or disadvantaged. Try to imagine the viewpoint of children and parents. Then make a list of factors that you think might disrupt communication.

You may have considered some of the following.

1. *Fear of information sharing*. Children and young people worry about who might find out about them. They may be concerned that you will tell their parents

what they have said. In any therapeutic relationship, some confidentiality is required so that the child feels safe enough to talk openly.

2. *Fear of being separated as a family.* Children and families often believe that working with services and disclosing information will result in a child or children being removed. In fact, much multi-agency work is preventative, supporting early identification of problems for effective solutions.

3. *Parental censorship.* Children may be told by their parents not to talk about issues to anyone outside the family home. It is useful to include in contracts and agreements parental permission for children to talk about anything they need to with their workers.

4. *Unexpected disclosure.* As a practitioner you can never be fully prepared for a child or young person disclosing something to you that you have never experienced before! However, remaining calm will help you to process what is being said and to gain some idea about what has happened.

5. *The adult–child relationship.* Children may have negative experiences of adults in their personal life and professionals. They are often seen as authoritative figures, who may or may not provide them with unwanted boundaries and do not listen to them.

6. *Negative experiences of professionals.* Families often have negative experiences of professionals, usually because they have felt let down by them or they did not follow through what they agreed to do. Parents may simply want to be left alone. Lack of knowledge and experience on the part of the practitioner, environmental factors beyond the professional's control, and unavoidable bad timing can also prevent effective communication in difficult circumstances.

Reflection point

It is important to consider the reasons why you, personally, may have difficulty in communicating in your professional practice with vulnerable children and young people. Make a brief list of factors about you (personality, attitude, experience) that may be relevant.

What would you do or say in your first contact with a family or young person to eradicate the negative experiences they hold of previous contacts with professionals? Make some bullet-point answers and then put them in order of priority.

Developing skills

By now you will have realized that the communication and interpersonal skills required to ensure a positive therapeutic interaction with a vulnerable or disadvantaged child or young person are both complex and vital. While theoretical frameworks and models can be applied to communication in such circumstances, practical communication styles and skills need to be developed through clinical practice.

Access to clinical supervision ensures that the practitioner has the opportunity to challenge and develop effective communication styles further. In addition, sensitive disclosures may be made by children and young people that may require evaluation by the practitioner, particularly if cultural values and norms are absent within the child's experience of family dynamics. Clinical supervision can strengthen reflective learning for both the novice and the experienced practitioner.

Interpreting and misinterpreting communication messages

Vignette   Interpreting communication messages: Gemma's story

Gemma, a 13-year-old girl, has lived with her father and stepmother since the age of 5 years. A residency order was sought for Gemma to reside with her father as a result of maternal substance misuse. Gemma's mother now lives in another county with a new partner and Gemma's half-siblings. Gemma absconded from home and school frequently, spending time with unknown adults. Professional concern about this behaviour led to a multi-agency meeting aimed at implementing a package of care to maintain Gemma's safety. Gemma did not articulate any reason for these behaviours, being unwilling to discuss them with professionals or family members. She did not communicate freely, appeared sullen and withdrawn, and averted her gaze and displayed poor eye contact when spoken to by adults. On occasion, Gemma demonstrated physical and verbal anger towards adults and peers.

Activity

Undertake the following five-minute exercise. With reference to the non-verbal communication cues listed above, could these be considered to be the typical attributes of communication with a teenager or signs of adverse emotional wellbeing? Provide three reasons for your conclusions.

In Gemma's story, the presence of such non-verbal cues may be misconstrued as communication barriers if the practitioner lacks knowledge about her circumstances. The multi-agency assessment drew upon the knowledge and skills of professionals from health, social care, and education. In partnership with Gemma and her family, they sought to resolve her risk-taking activities. A school-learning mentor who had a previous rapport with Gemma was recognized as being a positive role model and was in an ideal position to adopt the role of lead professional and advocate for Gemma. Within the context of this case study, communication techniques that were adopted included the provision of a neutral environment for meetings, with links to pleasurable activities not associated with the school or home environment. Gemma enjoyed music, and a local youth group provided a suitable venue and an area of shared enjoyment through which to develop a trusting rapport.

Generally, the lead professional adopted a relaxed communication style, while ensuring that sentences were short and not complex. Being alert to helpful potential seating arrangements and other environmental factors enhanced the chances of positive communication. The lead professional made eye contact with Gemma and paraphrased within the conversation to determine accuracy of understanding. Active listening techniques ensured that Gemma was able to express any anxieties. Over time, Gemma developed the skills and confidence to articulate her confusion and distress at being separated from her mother. Professionals were then able to source appropriate interventions to seek a positive resolution for Gemma and her family.

These findings are of value to practitioners working with vulnerable and disadvantaged children, regardless of the underlying triggers of such circumstances. The issues raised can provide reference points around which the practitioner can enhance practical communication skills and techniques to support vulnerable children and young people. Particular emphasis should be placed on observing nonverbal communication cues that a child or young person may demonstrate. While some children develop resilience to the impact of vulnerability and disadvantage, such life experiences may have significant impact upon a child's ability to develop social interactions and social reciprocity, and establish relationships with adults or peers. This can be challenging to both professionals and the young person. It is, therefore, essential that communication styles are tailored to provide an individualized response relevant to the interaction. This supports the notion of individualized care for children and young people.

Learning communication strategies for clinical practice

To deliver quality care to children and young people, it is important that effective communication skills are fostered. Communication can be categorized as verbal or non-verbal, with a combination of strategies being used within any social interaction. While theoretical frameworks and communication styles can be taught, practical experience and the opportunity to reflect upon particular scenarios from the practice environment are equally valuable learning resources.

Activity

What do you think are the necessary communication skills and attributes required of the practitioner to ensure that disadvantage and vulnerability do not prevent effective assessment and intervention? List three skills and three attributes. Then consider how you would incorporate and utilize these skills in your clinical practice.

Empathy, establishing rapport, gaining trust, active listening, and effective use of silence are all identified as being key skills and attributes to achieve optimum communication between individuals. Your communication skills will develop over time based upon experience, increased confidence as a practitioner, and access to opportunities to practise with supportive supervision.

It is paramount that children's nurses and others develop empathy and sensitivity in any given clinical situation. For vulnerable groups, there will be an increased need for such skills. Many children and young people may have been exposed to significant traumatic life experience that may not reflect the practitioner's personal experience or expectations. This further strengthens the requirement for effective peer and clinical supervision regardless of the level of competence of the practitioner.

Vignette   Assessment: Adam's story

Adam is 12 years old. He lives with his parents, both of whom are unemployed due to poor physical and mental health. The school health advisor has received a referral from teaching staff due to concerns regarding Adam's poor school attendance. The school has requested a health assessment as part of a wider multi-agency assessment to improve Adam's attendance and his academic attainment.

The school health advisor visited Adam at the family home. She found Adam to be monosyllabic, with flat intonation and generally unresponsive to direct questions. She felt that the interaction with Adam was awkward and stilted. She was unable to complete a comprehensive health assessment.

Activity

Write down three points that you would make if you had to report to Adam's multi-agency meeting.

What skills and attributes are required of the practitioner to ensure an optimal health assessment for Adam and his family? Take two minutes to list as many as you can.

Reflection point

- What communication techniques could be used to establish a positive interaction with Adam?
- Are there any particular strategies that the school health advisor could apply to the health assessment?

For the school health advisor, Adam's academic attainment had particular bearing upon the health assessment. A thorough assessment of Adam's social communication and cognitive development was requested via the multi-agency partners. The specialist speech and language therapist was able to complete a comprehensive assessment to support the multi-agency strategy. Subsequently, it was identified that Adam's cognitive development was much lower than anticipated for his chronological age, in part attributed to his poor school attendance. He had not accessed learning on a regular basis since the age of 6 years.

The school health advisor tailored her communication style to be effective in the health assessment. She adopted a communication style and approach that included simple terminology traditionally used with children of primary school age. She spoke clearly and simply, using an explicit sentence structure. To ensure that this was not demeaning or patronizing, she sought age-appropriate mediums and interests through which to complete the health assessment. This included meeting Adam away from the family home at an alternative venue of a local youth group, and capitalized on Adam's interests of snooker and PC games. Participation in shared interests supported Adam to build a trusting relationship with the school health advisor, an essential step to achieving optimum communication with children and young people.

The school health advisor was able to facilitate an effective environment in which Adam could gain the practitioner's trust. He was given time to communicate with the practitioner, who used active listening skills and paraphrasing throughout the health assessment. Adam developed the confidence to talk to the school health advisor and to express his thoughts and emotions. In turn, the school health advisor was able to facilitate a comprehensive health needs assessment. Adam was able to explore his emotions and, ultimately, a referral was brought forward for specialist mental health assessment. Adam explained that his low mood was due to the loss of a close family member some years previously.

Multi-agency measures were implemented within the school environment, as it also became apparent via the assessment that Adam avoided school due to embarrassment at his low academic attainment. The provision of resources to support communication has a positive role to play with children and young people and may include visual or pictorial tools or activities through which to articulate emotions, thoughts, and feelings. These can provide a conduit for children to explore personal emotions, particularly if articulation and expressive language difficulties are present. Vulnerable and disadvantaged children may not have the ability or insight to express how they may be feeling, so alternative ways to communicate are particularly valuable.

Establishing rapport and gaining trust are integral concepts to effective communication between children and professionals. For vulnerable children and young people, however, the development of effective relationships may be hindered by previous life experiences with either family members or professionals. With this in mind, it is of value to consider suitable strategies that enhance communication.

Vignette   Kim

Kim is an articulate 15-year-old and lives with foster parents. The looked-after children's (LAC) nurse is required to complete an annual health assessment, and contacts Kim's foster parents to arrange this.

Activity

> What are the key points that the LAC nurse should consider in anticipation of Kim's health assessment?

Although Kim was subject to a local authority care order, she was deemed to be competent to consent to the health assessment. The LAC nurse liaised directly with Kim to arrange a mutually convenient time and venue for the assessment. In this instance, text messaging was used to arrange the health assessment. While text messaging and email can be the preferred mode of communication for young people, the practitioner should be cautious. Although this form of communication can be useful for appointment reminders, young people may not respond to texts for a range of reasons, including a lack of 'credit' or a change of telephone number. Similarly, any telephone messages left on voicemail may not be retrieved. For data protection reasons, sensitive or personally identifiable data should not be shared electronically.

To facilitate an effective medium for communication, Kim chose the venue, which in this instance was a local burger bar. Being mindful of confidentiality within a public environment, the LAC nurse ensured that the consultation was within a private booth. Such measures may enhance the establishment of a trusting relationship between practitioner and client, supporting the notion of individualized patient care, with the patient being an active participant throughout the health assessment. Kim acknowledged that her wishes and opinions were accounted for throughout the assessment.

With knowledge of Kim's difficult life experiences, the LAC nurse allowed time for the therapeutic relationship to develop. Recognition of non-verbal communication cues assisted the practitioner to gauge the quality of the interaction. In practice, such assessments may require more than one consultation, but the value and effectiveness of establishing a trusting rapport has a positive impact on fostering meaningful child-centred health interventions and individualized care.

Vulnerability and disadvantage may impact upon an individual's ability to form relationships. Friendships with peers or trust in adults or professionals may be compromised because of previous experiences. Social interactions and reciprocity of communication can be limited if a child or young person has been subject to adverse social environments and experiences. The presentation of behaviour can differ greatly based upon life experiences. A young person may appear withdrawn and isolated. Challenging behaviours can be present. Often, these behaviours result from lack of trust or children's inability to express themselves effectively. However, the practitioner must avoid making generalizations in such circumstances. An individualized assessment and tailored approach to the consultation promote best practice.

The LAC nurse adopted a number of communication strategies to facilitate an effective consultation, including adequate, uninterrupted time for the meeting. Empathy and sensitivity were demonstrated within the consultation with the LAC nurse, and Kim was allowed time to express her thoughts and feelings. Kim was encouraged to express her emotions and anxieties. There was minimal distraction, despite the busy environment. The LAC nurse was alert to Kim's non-verbal communication cues, looking in particular for any signs of discomfort or anxiety.

A range of evidence-based resources and tools to aid effective assessment and communication are available for use with children and young people. Developed for use across a range of clinical settings, they are of particular value with vulnerable and disadvantaged groups. These are of significant benefit and will assist the practitioner to assess a young person's emotional well-being.

Conclusion

When engaging in any dialogue with children and families from vulnerable and disadvantaged circumstances, practitioners should be mindful of family dynamics and the role of parents and carers. It is feasible that carers may not be biologically related and traditional notions of family centred care or personal reflections on family dynamics may be challenged. Communication with parents of a vulnerable child may pose potential dilemmas for practitioners. It is important that practitioners remain objective about family situations and are not negatively influenced by preconceptions. The development of empathy towards adverse family situations may be challenging for a practitioner. Similarly, to facilitate effective therapeutic relationships, professionals should be aware of their own non-verbal communication cues and body language. Non-verbal cues of practitioner discomfort can be detrimental when trying to establish trust and rapport.

Key messages

- There are many reasons why children and young people are considered vulnerable or disadvantaged. However, information is available to guide practitioners.
- Gaining, sharing, and protecting information gleaned from and about children and young people can cause concern for nurses and other professionals, but central and local sources of information and guidance provide clear advice on decision-making.
- Skills and strategies for more effective communication with disadvantaged or vulnerable children and young people can be practised and refined by all those working in the field.

References

An Bord Altranais (2000) *The Code of Professional Conduct for Each Nurse and Midwife*. Dublin: An Bord Altranais.

Department for Children Schools and Families (2008) *Information Sharing: Guidance for Practitioners and Managers*. London: Department for Children Schools and Families.

Department for Children Schools and Families (2010) *Working Together to Safeguard Children*. London: The Stationery Office.

Department for Education and Skills (2003) *Every Child Matters*. London: The Stationery Office.

Department of Children and Youth Affairs (2011) *Children First: National Guidance for the Protection and Welfare of Children*. Dublin: Department of Children and Youth Affairs.

Department of Health (2009) *The Healthy Child Programme*. London: Department of Health.

Health Service Executive (2011) *Child Protection and Welfare: Practice Handbook*. Dublin: Health Service Executive.

Nursing and Midwifery Council (NMC) (2008) *Confidentiality*. London: NMC.

Ofsted (2008) *Safeguarding Children: The Third Joint Chief Inspectors' Report on Arrangements to Safeguard Children*. London: Ofsted.

Social Exclusion Task Force (2007) *Reaching Out: Think Family – Analysis and Themes from the Families at Risk Review*. London: Cabinet Office.

9 Children who have difficulty in communicating

Joanna Smith and Stacey Atkinson

This chapter addresses the needs of children who have difficulty in communicating. To care effectively for children who have difficulty in communicating, you will require knowledge and skills to understand the myths and preconceptions that impede effective engagement with a child with a communication difficulty; the challenges facing a child who has difficulty conveying his or her thoughts, feelings, and needs; and the range of methods available when communicating with a child with a communication difficulty. We will draw on three case studies (William, Sarah, and Haroon) to illustrate the complexity of caring for a child with a communication difficulty and the impact for them and their family.

Learning outcomes

After reading this chapter you should be able to:

1. Outline the reasons why a child or young person may have difficulty communicating
2. Reflect on the barriers that hinder effective engagement with a child or young person who has difficulty in communicating
3. Describe the methods available to assist you when communicating with a child or young person who has difficulty in communicating

---

Introduction

Language and speech development are central to effective verbal communication. *Speech* is the process of producing sound, while *language* is the ability to understand (receptive language) and use words in context (expressive language). Verbal communication difficulties occur when an individual has difficulty understanding and using speech and language. Disruption to one of the complex functional processes necessary for effective verbal communication can result in speech and language difficulties. This can impact on vocalizing words clearly or correctly, speaking fluently without hesitation or stuttering, using words and grammar correctly, formulating

Table 9.1 Types of speech and language difficulties

Category	Functional processes	Example of communication difficulties
Speech production	Coordination of the muscles and nerves involved in speech production	Absence of speech, stuttering, disturbances in the fluency of speech
	Formulating speech sounds	Imprecise or inconsistent speech
Morphology	Identifying the meaning of words	Misuse of words, tenses, numbers, gender
Phonology	The function of sounds within a language	Unable to identify the meaning of voice tone such as a rise in intonation to indicate a question
Semantics	Structure of speech	Poor flow of topics in conversation
	Literal meaning	Naming and word-finding problems
	Figurative meaning	Misunderstands idioms, e.g. figures of speech or sayings
Syntax	Rules for the formation of grammar	Confusion about who does what within a sentence
Pragmatics	Speech acts	Responses do not match those of the previous speaker
	Affective messages	Misunderstands communications such as emotional tone

Source: Adapted from Dennis (2010)

sentences that make sense to others, and understanding others (Dennis 2010) (see Table 9.1). In addition, an inability to respond to non-verbal communication, such as facial expression, the use of hand gestures, and body language, can result in misinterpretation of verbal communications.

Estimating the number of children with communication difficulties is complex because there is no accepted definition of communication difficulties, and the range of such difficulties is diverse and variable in the way in which they present (Simeonsson 2003; Enderby and Pickstone 2005). Reasons for a child having communication difficulties include:

- primarily language acquisition failure of unknown cause, often referred to as specific language impairment;
- developmental disorders where there is an abnormality in the development of brain structures and functions;

- communication difficulties associated with sensory losses, such as impaired hearing and vision;
- acquired communication difficulties following damage to the brain; for example, as a consequence of seizure disorders and traumatic brain injury;
- communication difficulties associated with complex or long-term health needs; for example, speech production may be affected when a child has a tracheotomy because exhaled air by-passes the vocal cords.

Autism

Vignette   Autism: William's case

William, aged 8, has a diagnosis of autism that has resulted in specific communication needs. William does not communicate verbally. An example of an everyday challenge for William is highlighted below.

William would like to play with a specific spinning toy kept in a locked cupboard. He leads different people by the hand to the cupboard, but no one knows that he wants a toy from inside the cupboard. William gradually becomes more frustrated. He places his hands over his ears and hums loudly, progressing next to digging his nails into the hands of people he connects with, and then he starts kicking the cupboard. Gradually, those near William move away, and he is left alone. He sits in a corner and sobs. He refuses to look at anyone for the rest of the day and will not accept food or drink.

Reflection point

Reflect on your own practice. If you were working with William, how would you encourage him to re-engage with you and his environment?

Autism is one of a number of developmental disorders collectively known as autistic spectrum disorders (ASD). Autistic spectrum disorders affect individuals in different ways and are characterized by a triad of impairments that affect communication, imagination, and social interaction (Wing and Gould 1979). Many children with ASD do not interact through speech (National Autistic Society 2007). This has been attributed to localized cerebral abnormalities in several regions of the brain, including the frontal and temporal lobes and cerebellum, resulting in poor or no speech development and a reduced ability to appreciate the social context of speech (McGregor *et al.* 2008). Children with ASD often communicate through non-verbal behaviour, like William when he was unable to communicate a desire to play with the toy from the cupboard. For children with ASD who have developed speech, speech has noticeable characteristics such as echolalia – repeating speech made by another person, or the child may become fixated on the topic rather than the interactions that occur within conversations (Frith 2003).

Children with ASD may show very little or no interest in imaginative play, often viewing the world in concrete terms (Atwood 2006). There is a tendency to prefer rigid routines that can appear to others as excessive and obsessive. A change of routine or new experiences such as a hospital admission or health appointment can be extremely disruptive and disturbing for a child with ASD. The child may have difficulty in transferring information and experiences from previous situations to new ones (Dickenson and Hannah 2007). In addition, meeting people who do not understand their way of communicating can be frightening and frustrating for the child.

Many children with ASD have difficulty engaging in social interactions (Happe 1994). They may distance themselves purposely from other people. Social interactions are typified by a lack of eye contact. For children who are able to interact socially, attempts at communicating may not conform to expected norms, such as staring, using rushed or slow speech, and a perceived lack of empathy or understanding of others' feelings or ideas.

Children with ASD may have different sensory perceptions to other people. Sensory perceptions can be enhanced or reduced, including touch pressure, vision, movement and balance, hearing, taste and smell, which can impact on their experiences and interpretation of their environment (Myles *et al.* 2005). For example, William's tendency to place his hands over his ears when hearing intense noise suggests altered hearing perception. Many children with ASD are acutely aware of smell, actively smelling objects or environments (Myles *et al.* 2005). It is important that sensory needs are considered when engaging with a child with ASD. When a child with ASD is intensely focused on an activity, they can become mesmerized with the activity and may not respond to other environmental cues (Williams 2001). Other children may be highly sensitive, and an external stimulus can break their concentration, which can result in the activity being abandoned. Understanding a child's specific sensory needs assists in effective engagement and building a relationship with the child through appreciating their perspective of their environment.

Congenital cytomegalovirus

Vignette   Cytomegalovirus: Sarah's case

> Sarah, aged 10, has profound hearing loss caused by cytomegalovirus. She is one of four children and lives at home with her parents. She attends a specialist school for deaf children, which she enjoys, and is achieving high standards in her schoolwork. Sarah communicates fluently using lip reading and British Sign Language. She is sociable and has a wide circle of hearing and hearing-impaired friends. Sarah's recent hospital admission was not a positive experience.

She was admitted to hospital with acute abdominal pain. The ward staff struggled to interact with Sarah, who felt isolated from the other children. This resulted in her parents juggling work and caring for their other children to ensure that one parent was always present with Sarah while she was in hospital, acting as an interpreter for health professionals when they engaged with Sarah. Sarah had a good relationship with her parents but was embarrassed by their presence – parents of other children of similar age were not continually present on the ward. The nurses were reliant on the parents to communicate with Sarah, which inadvertently resulted in Sarah often being excluded from interactions. Lack of ability to communicate with Sarah was not consistent with providing child-centred care. Ultimately, the health professionals were unable to appreciate fully Sarah's emotional and psychological needs.

Reflection point

Reflect on your own practice. How would you have included Sarah when undertaking a pain assessment?

Cytomegalovirus (CMV) is a member of the herpes virus group, which has the ability to remain dormant within the body over a long period. Cytomegalovirus is a common virus and is spread through intimate contact with a person excreting the virus in their saliva, urine, breast milk or other bodily fluids. For most healthy persons who acquire CMV, there are few symptoms and no long-term health consequences. However, the virus can be transmitted *in utero* to an unborn child, which for some children can have significant consequences, including impaired hearing, and learning or physical disabilities (Adler 1992). Congenital CMV infection is a leading cause of hearing loss in young children (Fowler et al. 1997).

Cerebral palsy

Vignette   Cerebral palsy: Haroon's case

Haroon, aged 15, has cerebral palsy associated with being born prematurely. Haroon has learning and physical disabilities and is prescribed anticonvulsant medication to manage his epilepsy and medication for excessive drooling, which he is unable to control. Haroon has a range of care needs.

Haroon is incontinent and needs support with intimate care. He has limited movement, particularly in his lower limbs, although his ability to use an electric wheelchair provides him with some independence. Haroon has never developed speech but can communicate through sounds. For example, he makes loud noises when happy or listening to music and cries when unhappy. Haroon's care has been inconsistent, and he has not been provided with the opportunity to use augmentative communication methods, primarily because of negative assumptions about his abilities as a consequence of having cerebral palsy. Haroon has lived in a range of local authority care settings since he was 2 years of age. He has recently been re-housed and is living in a residential home for young people with physical and learning disabilities. He has become withdrawn and refuses to communicate.

Reflection point

Reflect on your own practice. How would you assist Haroon to adapt and interact with his peers in his new environment?

Cerebral palsy is a term used to describe a group of disorders that affect body movement, balance, and posture (Reddihough and Collins 2003). Cerebral palsy occurs when non-progressive damage to the immature brain adversely affects its normal development. Prenatal causes of cerebral palsy include cerebral haemorrhage, infections such CMV, and, less commonly, environmental factors such as excessive maternal alcohol intake during pregnancy. Birth complications can compromise oxygen delivery to the baby resulting in hypoxic brain damage, while post-natal causes of cerebral palsy include traumatic head injury, infections such as meningitis, and brain haemorrhage (Reddihough and Collins 2003). The impact of cerebral palsy on the child depends on the severity of the condition, socio-economic factors, access to care interventions, and service provision (Beckung *et al.* 2008). Cerebral palsy may involve muscle stiffness, poor muscle tone, uncontrolled movements and problems with posture, balance, coordination, walking, speech, swallowing, breathing, hearing and vision, and continence. Like Haroon, many children with cerebral palsy have associated conditions such as epilepsy and learning difficulties.

Learning disability

A learning disability is defined as a 'reduced ability to understand new or complex information' because of intellectual impairment or delayed development (Department of Health 2001: 14). Children with learning disabilities are likely to require support to undertake activities of daily living appropriate to their age and stage of

Table 9.2 Spectrum of learning disabilities

Mild	Moderate	Profound
Can communicate verbally but comprehension of spoken words may be limited	Verbal communication limited, restricted vocabulary, and poor comprehension of spoken words	Limited ability to interact with others, may not develop verbal communication skills, and limited understanding of the spoken word
Develops some literacy and numeracy skills, usually able to read and write, again comprehension may be limited	Limited development of literacy and numeracy skills	Usually unable to read and write
Usually develop sufficient skills to lead an independent life	Skills in self-care often achieved but there is some dependence on others	Often unable to develop self-care skills; highly dependent on others

Source: Adapted from Burke and Cigno (2000)

development, and will have difficulty in social functioning. Learning disabilities are diverse in terms of the impact on the child's ability to communicate verbally and achieve independent living (Table 9.2).

Many children with a learning disability have difficulty in communicating. For the child with mild or moderate disabilities, expressive language skills may be more advanced than receptive language. This can be problematic, as assumptions are often made about a child's level of understanding based on their expressive language skills. Communicating with children with more profound learning disabilities is particularly challenging, and there is potential for such children to be excluded from usual nurse–patient interactions during care provision. It is important for the nurse caring for a child with profound learning disability to consider ways to build up an effective relationship to interact with the child. Otherwise, the nurse, albeit unwittingly, may fail to meet the child's individual needs.

The level of support required by a child with learning disability to meet their intellectual, health, self-care, and social care needs is variable. The National Service Framework (Department of Health 2004a) Standard 8, and Section 12.6 of the Report of Disability Policy Review (Department of Health 2011), relate specifically to disabled children and young people and those with complex health needs, and recognize the uniqueness of each child. To ensure that the child and family receive the best support available, professionals across service provision must work together. Services (health, social care, and education) must be coordinated and care packages individually designed. Services must be centred on the specific needs of the child and family, and reviewed at key transitional stages in the child's development. Service and care delivery must be undertaken in collaboration with the child and family.

Engaging with children who have difficulty communicating

Activity

Read the vignettes of William, Sarah, and Haroon again. William, Sarah, and Haroon have diverse communication difficulties and needs. However, all were isolated because of their difficulty with communicating.

What factors do you think contributed to the lack of engagement by nurses and other professionals with William, Sarah, and Haroon?

One of the key features in the three vignettes relates to the isolation that all three children experienced as a result of having difficulty communicating, a consequence of which was that their immediate needs were not addressed. Failure to listen to the child contravenes their fundamental right to be heard (United Nations 1989). Irish and UK legislation and policy guidance across education, health, and social services advocates that professionals must consult with children, including children with disabilities, about decisions that affect them (Department of Health 1991, 2004a, 2004b, 2007; Department for Education and Skills/Department of Health 2005; Social Services Inspectorate and Children's Research Centre 2006).

Training is available to help professionals to develop the skills required to maintain communication with children who have difficulties (Marchant and Gordon 2001). Despite legislation and the availability of training, evidence suggests that there are recurring failures in the implementation of policy imperatives in practice. Good practice in relation to communicating with children who have disabilities is limited, and the children perceive that they do not have a voice (Stone 2001; Cavet and Sloper 2004; Mitchell et al. 2009).

Consulting with disabled children

A range of projects have been undertaken with children with learning disabilities or who have difficulty communicating with the explicit aim of exploring children's views about being listened to and valued (Stone 2001; Mitchell et al. 2009). Findings from these projects highlight that children want to be respected and to have a say in things that matter to them. Children have reported that adults, including professionals, do not listen and do not try to communicate with them, and that communication aids are not always available in different aspects of their lives, thus hindering their participation in wider society. Children with learning disabilities or difficulties communicating say:

- Talk directly to us, not just our parents, or our carers.
- Make sure you really understand us because I have seen carers, parents, and other people who didn't even know or can't be bothered to find out how we say 'yes' or 'no'.

- We do have feelings.
- Show an interest in us; make it more than just a job.
- We're just like other children.

Barriers to engaging with children who have difficulty in communicating

Activity

Think for a few minutes about what may cause professionals to engage inadequately with children who have difficulty in communicating. Try to list three reasons and then check the list below.

Many factors contribute to professionals' lack of engagement with children and young people who have difficulty in communicating. These include the following.

- Verbal communication is the dominant means by which people communicate. Individuals who communicate primarily by the use of signs, symbols or behaviours are in the minority and at risk of exclusion (Mitchell *et al.* 2009).
- Professionals may lack the knowledge, skills, experience, and confidence to communicate effectively with children with a disability or who have difficulty in communicating (Joseph Rowntree Foundation 1999).
- Professionals may fail to take the time to engage actively with children who have difficulty in communicating and therefore do not listen to their views (Marchant and Gordon 2001; Stone 2001).
- Professionals may display negative attitudes and prejudices when working with children who have difficulty in communicating (Marchant and Gordon 2001).
- Inclusion is restricted by the views of children who are articulate becoming the dominant voice (Burke and Cigno 2000).
- The use of interpreters has the potential to misrepresent the views of children who have difficulty in communicating (Burke and Cigno 2000).
- Diagnostic overshadowing may occur, as outlined below (Mason and Scior 2004).

There is no easy way to engage meaningfully with a child who has limited means of communicating. Prejudice can result in discriminatory practices (Marchant and Gordon 2001). Key to overcoming barriers when engaging with a child who has difficulty communicating is for you to recognize that communication is a two-way process. You must take responsibility for providing the child with the opportunity to express their views (Marchant and Gordon 2001). This can be achieved by being committed to finding out about the child's individual means of communication and ensuring that adequate time is made available to listen to the child (Burke and Cigno 2000).

Diagnostic overshadowing

Diagnostic overshadowing occurs when the needs of the child are assumed to be based on their diagnosis rather than based on an assessment of their abilities (Mason and Scior 2004). Diagnostic overshadowing results in the stereotyping of children who have difficulty communicating, usually because of lack of experience and knowledge on the part of professionals or carers. There is a perception that the child will behave in a specific way because of the diagnosis. Consider the needs of Haroon, who will point to objects and make noises to attract attention as a means of communicating his needs. Given the opportunity, Haroon may have benefited from using augmentative communication methods, but these were not considered because of diagnostic overshadowing. It was assumed that Haroon, because of a diagnosis of cerebral palsy, would not be able to learn alternative methods of communication, which ultimately prevented him from experiencing greater opportunities to interact more effectively and to explore his environment. Yet Haroon clearly has the ability to differentiate between pleasant and unpleasant experiences, and to identify his needs: a prerequisite to learning augmentative communication systems.

Diagnostic overshadowing can also occur when a child displays behaviours that challenge normal expectations. For example, behaviours such as 'head banging' can be associated with a learning disability but can also be one way for a child to communicate. To the uninformed, the child's needs may not be recognized. A child may be trying to indicate that they are in pain, but due to diagnostic overshadowing this is interpreted as a behavioural problem rather than a means of communicating.

Another result of diagnostic overshadowing is that the child may have unmet needs, and the nurse is at risk of negligence through a lack of understanding of the way in which the child communicates. You can overcome diagnostic overshadowing by being aware of the impact of making assumptions about a child's ability based on their diagnosis, and by undertaking a detailed assessment of the child's needs including the way the child communicates. It is likely that Haroon did not have a detailed assessment in relation to his communication skills and so the opportunity for him to develop more effective communication methods was lost.

Assessing a child's communication abilities

Children with communication difficulties require detailed visual, hearing, and developmental assessments. They must be referred to speech and language services and learning disability nursing services. The aims of speech and language services include the provision of specialist assessment and diagnostic services for children and the provision of education and training to parents and other members of the multidisciplinary team to ensure that children receive effective, consistent, and appropriate support (RCSLT 2006; IASLT 2007). Speech and language therapy aims to develop the social, cognitive, and motor skills that contribute to effective communication and to ensure that interventions are appropriate to each child and their environment (RCSLT 2006; IASLT 2007). This is often achieved with the use of communication aids.

Undertaking a detailed assessment of the child's needs begins the process of systematically planning individualized care. For a child who has difficulty communicating, identifying the child's specific communication needs is not only central to effective care delivery but essential if the child is to be valued as an individual and engaged in care decisions (as appropriate to their age and stage of development).

Activity

Imagine that you are to undertake an assessment of a child's communication ability and needs. (Assume that you have observed signs that they may have difficulty in this area.) What issues would you take into account? Take a few minutes to think and to make a list.

You may have thought about:

- involving, where possible, the child in the assessment process;
- identifying how the child usually communicates both verbally and non-verbally and whether there has been a change to their method of communicating;
- documenting specific communication challenges. For example, verbal language may not be possible, or speech may become hesitant or repetitive when the child is distressed or in an unfamiliar environment;
- documenting the use and meaning of non-verbal communication, including the meaning of any specific eye movements;
- identifying the child's preferences and reactions to the proximity of others and the use of touch. Some children with ASD evade close physical contact. In contrast, children with sensory impairment may use physical contact as a form of reassurance;
- identifying any senses that the child uses to communicate. Visually or hearing-impaired children may use smell as a way of being aware of their environment.

As with all children, it is important for the nurse to provide explanations about the care to be given in advance of the event. When a child has difficulty in communicating, additional thought and imagination, appropriate to the child, may be required to ensure that the child understands the care being planned. For example, when a child uses smell as a way of interacting with their environment, allowing the child to smell the soap could be used to communicate that washing is the care activity to be undertaken. Scents such as perfumes, if used consistently, may help children discriminate between staff. Children who are visually impaired and those who are auditory-sensitive may use hearing to identify cues from the environment. This means that surprise actions can be frightening and distressing for the child. The nurse should communicate verbally and, where possible and if appropriate, use augmentative communication systems. The assistance of a learning disabilities nurse or speech therapist should be sought to enhance the effectiveness of communication.

Practical tips when communicating with a child who has difficulty in communicating

- Find out how the child usually communicates.
- Ensure that the child recognizes that they are being spoken to. Say the child's name clearly and establish eye contact where possible.
- Use language carefully to explain who you are and, when appropriate, the care that you are going to be undertaking.
- Be consistent in the use of verbal and non-verbal modes of communication.
- Use clear and unambiguous language: short, simple sentences are easier to understand than long, convoluted sentences.
- Ensure clarity in pronunciation of words and be consistent in voice tone.
- Do not try new ways of communicating that might confuse or alienate a child once you have adopted an efficient communication system.
- Be non-directive and reflect the child's attempts at communication back to clarify you have understood what they are trying to tell you.
- Allow sufficient time for the child to respond. Communicate at the child's pace.

Methods of communication for children who have difficulty in communicating

A range of methods of communication is available for children who have difficulty in communicating. Children often use traditional methods such as speech in conjunction with non-verbal aids, known as augmentative communication. Everyone uses augmentative communication techniques. For example, when it is difficult to communicate verbally because of a noisy environment, gestures, exaggerated facial expressions and, more recently, text messaging are often used to augment spoken words. Children with limited speech, like William, often augment verbal sounds with the use of communication aids, such as pictures and language boards.

Signing

Sign language is used widely within deaf communities. It is a rich and diverse visual language, constantly evolving with its own grammar, idioms and dialects, and varies around the globe (e.g. British Sign Language (BSL), Irish Sign Language, American Sign Language). BSL involves using signs that represent words, or finger spelling when there is no universal sign available. Finger spelling is an intrinsic part of BSL, and within the UK involves using both hands (in Ireland one hand is used) to make different shapes that represent letters of the alphabet, enabling words to be constructed. Finger spelling is a useful skill because it can be used across a number of signing systems. Many children, like Sarah, use BSL. Staff experienced in signing will be able to communicate with children who use BSL as their method of communication. When the nurse cannot communicate with the child, deaf support services and interpreters should be used to ensure that the child is involved in care and care decisions. BSL assumes a basic level of language and literacy skills. Makaton is a form of signing that uses symbols together with speech, where possible, to visually represent words (Marchant and Gordon 2001). It is suitable for children with learning disabilities who have communication, language, and literacy problems because it uses a small nucleus vocabulary associated with everyday activities.

Pictures, photographs, symbols, and objects of reference

Pictures, photographs, symbols, and objects of reference are methods of communication widely used by children (Marchant and Gordon 2001). Objects of reference are real objects that can be used by the child or carer to indicate a need or impending activity. The use of real objects may be of value when the child has poor vision and may be reliant on tactile senses. For example, a fork may be used to communicate the need for lunch, a key to represent a drive in the car, and a face cloth to represent washing. Often, 'miniature' objects that the child commonly uses are placed in a box, which enables the child to carry the objects with them. Objects of reference are typically used with children with significant communication difficulties and severe learning disabilities who may not be able to manipulate more advanced communication systems.

Communication can be achieved using pictures, photographs, and symbols. Pictures and symbols differ in that the former is an image of an object, whereas symbols are more abstract and a representation of an object word or activity. Figure 9.1

Figure 9.1 Examples of picture and symbol cards

provides an example of picture communication symbols. Picture communication can use pictures, photographs, and symbols, which, in their most simplistic form, can be used by the child or carer to indicate a need or impending activity. Commercial versions of more than 4000 cards are available, representing a wide range of objects and emotions. Picture communication symbols tend to be more intuitive. Such symbols can be easily identified even by people not familiar with the communication system, compared with other symbol communication methods such as Blissymbols (Fuller and Lloyd 1991). Blissymbols is an international comprehensive language based on symbols, and although the symbols are often abstract in nature they can be used to communicate complex ideas.

Photographs can be used as an alternative to pictures. The choice of photograph needs careful consideration because they are often not uniform in size or colour and, if the photograph captures a range of images, the child may become confused about what the image is portraying.

Picture communication symbols can be used to create picture exchange communication systems (PECS) and visual timetables. PECS is a method of teaching children to communicate by exchanging information on cue cards until the desired result is achieved. For example, the child could hold up a card depicting an object requesting a drink, but the picture can be changed to represent different types of drink (milk, juice, water) (Baker 2007). The process of learning is achieved through positive reinforcement when the desired outcome is achieved. PECS provides the child with greater autonomy in communicating their needs.

Visual timetables are a way of outlining the day's plans to the child. They are widely used in education but can be adapted to healthcare settings. Pictures, photographs or symbols are placed in sequential order of the day's events; for example, 8 am breakfast with a picture of breakfast, 9 am bath time with a picture of a bath, and 10 am doctor's round with a picture of doctor. Using pictures with Velcro backing enables them to be removed when events have occurred, keeping the child up-to-date as the day unfolds. An example of a visual timetable is presented in Figure 9.2.

Pictures or photographs are particularly useful in care settings. They can be placed in key areas such as the toilet, toy cupboard, and play areas, enabling the child to become familiar with their environment and staff. Good practice would include exploring the environment and showing the child the pictures during the admission process.

Activity

Think of a child that you know (with or without difficulty communicating), and make a visual timetable for them. Discuss your work with a colleague and see if the images could be simpler or more obvious. Test it out with the child, if possible, to see if they understand it.

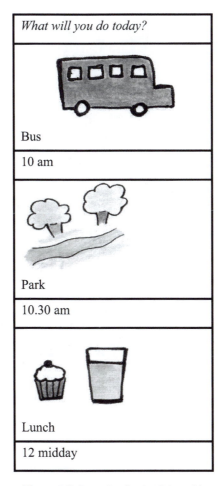

Figure 9.2 Example of a visual timetable

Individual methods of communicating

A large part of everyday interactions occurs through non-verbal communication (Rungapadiatry 2004). Children who have difficulty communicating are even more likely to rely on non-verbal communication. This will be the only method of communicating for children for whom language is not possible. Non-verbal communication can be subtle. For example, eye movements can be used to express a need or answer a question (eye deviation to the left may means 'no', eye deviation to the right means 'yes'), and a grimace might reveal pain or unhappiness. These subtle attempts to communicate can easily be missed by a nurse if he or she is busy and does not understand the way in which the child communicates.

Intensive individual interaction is a method of communicating with children who have a more profound communication difficulty and learning disability (Caldwell 1998). It relies on understanding subtle cues used by the child to communicate, and can be compared with the way in which a parent interacts with an infant prior to the development of verbal language. The parent responds to the sounds, babble, noises, and body language of the infant to understand and meet the infant's needs. The reciprocal interaction encourages both the parent and infant to continue communicating, which enhances mutual understanding. For a child with significant difficulty communicating, achieving eye contact can be essential to engagement. Intensive interaction requires the responder to be highly observant in realizing the possible connections to be made and being open to entering the child's world. It involves a significant time commitment and, while its use is possible in some settings, it is not possible during short encounters with the child, such as acute hospital admissions.

Communicating through behaviours

All behaviours, until proved otherwise, should be assumed to be an attempt by the child to communicate (Morris 1998). Behaviours, such as those demonstrated by William, are often labelled as challenging because they are challenging for individuals who come into contact with the child. A significant number of individuals with a learning disability exhibit behaviours that are challenging (Mansell *et al.* 2002), often expressed verbally (shouting, screaming, inappropriate language), physically or sexually and directed at themselves, others or inanimate objects. Although episodes of challenging behaviour can be frightening and disturbing, it is important to realize the child is trying to communicate. The practitioner needs to analyse the possible reasons for the behaviour – is the child in pain, anxious or lonely?

Conclusion

This chapter has highlighted the challenges faced by children with communication difficulties. Through William, Sarah, and Haroon's stories of isolation, practical advice has been provided that will enable you to reflect on your own practice and consider actions that you would take if faced with a similar situation.

Key messages

- Children have a right to be heard irrespective of their ability or inability to communicate with ease. Negative attitudes and prejudice are major contributing factors preventing professionals from interacting with children who have difficulty communicating.
- Diagnostic overshadowing can result in the child's potential not being fully realized. Challenging behaviours are often an attempt by the child to communicate.

- Developing a therapeutic relationship with the child requires effective child–nurse interactions. A range of communication methods is available to support children who have difficulty communicating.

References

Adler, S. (1992) Cytomegalovirus and pregnancy, *Current Opinion in Obstetrics and Gynaecology*, 4(5): 670–5.
Atwood, T. (2006) *Why Does Chris Do That?* London: National Autistic Society.
Baker, S. (2007) *Approaches to Autism*. Norwich: National Autistic Society.
Beckung, E., White-Koning, M., Macelli, M., McManus, M., Michelsen, S., Parkers, J. *et al.* (2008) Health status of children with cerebral palsy living in Europe: a multi-centre study, *Child: Care, Health and Development*, 34(6): 806–14.
Burke, P. and Cigno, K. (2000) *Learning Disabilities in Children*. Oxford: Blackwell Science.
Caldwell, P. (1998) *Communication with People with Profound Learning Disability and Extra Special Needs*. Brighton: Pavilion.
Cavet, J. and Sloper, P. (2004) The participation of children and young people in decisions about UK service development, *Child: Care, Health and Development*, 34(6): 806–14.
Dennis, M. (2010) Language disorders in children with central nervous system injury, *Journal of Clinical and Experimental Neuropsychology*, 33(4): 417–32.
Department for Education and Skills/Department of Health (2005) *Working Together to Safeguard Children: A Guide to Interagency Working to Safeguard and Promote the Welfare of Children*. London: The Stationery Office.
Department of Health (1991) *The Children Act 1989*. London: The Stationery Office.
Department of Health (2001) *Valuing People: A New Strategy for Learning Disabilities for the 21st Century*. London: The Stationery Office.
Department of Health (2004a) *National Service Framework for Children, Young People and Maternity Services: Disabled Children and Young People and those with Complex Health Needs*. London: The Stationery Office.
Department of Health (2004b) *The Children Act 2004*. London: The Stationery Office.
Department of Health (2007) *Services for People with Learning Disabilities and Challenging Behaviour or Mental Health Needs (Mansell Report)*. London: The Stationery Office.
Department of Health (2011) *Report of Disability Policy Review: Expert Reference Group on Disability Policy*. Dublin: Department of Health.
Dickenson, P. and Hannah, L. (2007) *It Can Get Better. Dealing with Common Behavioural Problems in Young Children with Autism: A Guide for Parents and Carers*. London: National Autistic Society.
Enderby, P. and Pickstone, C. (2005) How many people have communication disorders and why does it matter?, *Advances in Speech and Language Pathology*, 7(1): 464–75.
Fowler, K.B., McCollister, F.P., Dahle, A.J., Boppana, S., Britt W.J. and Pass, R.F. (1997) Progressive and fluctuating sensorineural hearing loss in children with asymptomatic congenital cytomegalovirus infection, *Journal of Pediatrics*, 130: 624–30.
Frith, U. (2003) *Autism: Explaining the Enigma*, 2nd edn. Oxford: Blackwell Publishing.
Fuller, D. and Lloyd, L. (1991) Toward a common usage of iconicity terminology, *Augmentative and Alternative Communication*, 7: 215–20.
Happe, F. (1994) *Autism: An Introduction to the Psychological Theory*. London: UCL Press.
Irish Association of Speech and Language Therapists (IASLT) (2007) *Specific Speech and Language Impairment in Children: Definition, Service Provision and Recommendations for Change*. Dublin: IASLT.

Joseph Rowntree Foundation (1999) *Supporting Disabled Children and their Families*. York: Joseph Rowntree Foundation.

Mansell, J., Ashman, B., Macdonald, S. and Beadle-Brown, J. (2002) Residential care in the community for adults with intellectual disability: needs, characteristics and services, *Journal of Intellectual Disability*, 46(8): 625–33.

Marchant, R. and Gordon, R. (2001) *Two-way Street: Communicating with Disabled Children and Young People – Handbook*. Leicester: NSPCC.

Mason, J. and Scior, K. (2004) Diagnostic overshadowing amongst clinicians working with people with intellectual disability in the UK, *Journal of Applied Research in Intellectual Disability*, 17: 85–90.

McGregor, E., Nunez, M., Cebula, K. and Gomez, J. (2008) *Autism: An Integrated View from Neurocognitive, Clinical and Intervention Research*. Oxford: Blackwell.

Mitchell, W., Franklin, A., Greco, V. and Bell, M. (2009) Working with children with learning disabilities and/or who communicate non-verbally: research experiences and their implications for social work education, increased participation and social inclusion, *Social Work Education*, 28(3): 309–24.

Morris, J. (1998) *Don't Leave Us Out*. York: Joseph Rowntree Foundation.

Myles, B., Cook, K., Miller, N., Rinner, L. and Robbins, L. (2005) *Asperger Syndrome and Sensory Issues: Practical Solutions for Making Sense of the World*. Shawnee Mission, KS: Autism Asperger Publishing Company.

National Autistic Society (NAS) (2007) *Approaches to Autism: An Easy to Use Guide to Many and Varied Approaches to Autism*. London: NAS.

Reddihough, D.S. and Collins, K.J. (2003) The epidemiology and causes of cerebral palsy, *Australian Journal of Physiotherapy*, 49: 7–12.

Royal College of Speech and Language Therapists (RCSLT) (2006) *Communicating Quality 3. RCSLT's Guidance on Best Practice in Service Organisation and Provision*. London: RCSLT.

Rungapadiatry, D. (2004) *Interpersonal Communication and Psychology for Healthcare Professionals*. London: Butterworth-Heinemann.

Simeonsson, R.J. (2003) Classification of communication disabilities in children: contribution of the International Classification on Functioning, Disability and Health, *International Journal of Audiology*, 342: S2–S8.

Social Services Inspectorate and Children's Research Centre (2006) *Consulting with Children with Disabilities as Service Users: Practical and Methodological Considerations*. Dublin: Social Services Inspectorate and Children's Research Centre.

Stone, E. (2001) *Consulting with Disabled Children and Young People*. York: Joseph Rowntree Foundation.

United Nations (1989) *Convention on the Rights of the Child*. Geneva: United Nations.

Williams, D. (2001) *Autism and Sensing: The Unlost Instinct*. London: Jessica Kingsley.

Wing, L. and Gould, J. (1979) Severe impairments of social interaction of associated abnormalities in children: epidemiology and classification, *Journal of Autism and Developmental Disorders*, 9: 11–29.

10 Legal and ethical dimensions of communicating with children and their families

Ursula Kilkelly and Eileen Savage

This chapter outlines the legal and ethical framework governing the relationship between healthcare professionals, child patients and their parents. It identifies the legal requirements regarding consent to a child's medical treatment in order to highlight the issues for communication practices in this area. Practical assistance is provided to help you work with children and families within this legal framework.

Learning outcomes

By the end of this chapter you should be able to:

1. Understand the law governing the giving of consent in respect of children's medical treatment
2. Identify the broad legal and ethical principles governing communication with children and families in the healthcare setting, and apply these principles in the effective communication with children and their families
3. Avoid conflict with parents in the provision of health care to their children

---

Introduction

Law sets important parameters for how children are treated by healthcare professionals and so an awareness of what the law requires is an essential part of good healthcare practice. The requirement to obtain consent to medical interventions derives from the recognition of the individual's right to autonomy or self-determination (Donnelly 2002). In most cases, medical intervention without legal consent will constitute an unlawful interference with the patient's body for which the healthcare professional may be held legally responsible. Legal protection of the right to autonomy presumes that the patient is an adult with full mental capabilities. The right to autonomy applies in a different way when the patient is a child; consent is still important but somebody acting on behalf of the patient – often the child's parent – may have the power to give legal consent (Kilkelly and Donnelly 2007).

Nurses' interactions with children and their families are also guided by an ethical or moral framework of 'what ought to be' grounded in the principles of beneficence (to do good), non-maleficence (to do no harm), autonomy, justice (fair and equal treatment of others), veracity (to tell the truth), and fidelity (to keep one's promise) (Beauchamp and Childress 2009). Accordingly, nurses have both an ethical and a legal 'duty of care' to act in the best interests of children and families. This 'duty of care' is inherently linked with standards of performance and codes of professional conduct published by regulatory bodies of the nursing profession in individual countries.

Activity

- What is your understanding of your 'duty of care' to act in the best interests of children and families when communicating with them?
- How does the regulatory body of the nursing profession in your country define 'duty of care'?

The legal framework

Each legal framework is different. In Ireland, the issue of consent to medical treatment is dealt with by a single provision of a statute that entitles a child over 16 years to consent to medical treatment. The law currently offers no guidance on the capacity of children under 16 years to consent to medical treatment; nor does it offer guidance on when a child may refuse to consent. In such cases, principles must be drawn from professional codes of practice and, in extreme cases, the Constitution of Ireland (Bunreacht na hEireann) as applied by the courts. In England and Wales, the courts have been actively filling these gaps, as outlined later. What both jurisdictions have in common is the international legal framework, including the European Convention on Human Rights (ECHR), which has effect in the United Kingdom by virtue of the Human Rights Act 1998 and in Ireland by the ECHR Act 2003. Also important is the United Nations Convention on the Rights of the Child (CRC; United Nations 1989) to which both Ireland and the UK are parties. This provides a holistic framework for the treatment of children and enshrines four general principles that should inform all decision-making concerning children, including in the healthcare setting: the right to life, survival, and development (Article 6); the right to enjoy Convention rights without discrimination (Article 2); the requirement that the child's best interests are a primary consideration in all actions affecting the child (Article 3); and the right of the child to have his/her views taken into account in all matters concerning him/her (Article 12). The CRC has been supplemented by the European Guidelines on Child-friendly Healthcare, adopted in 2011 by the Council of Europe. Based on the Convention's four general principles, the Guidelines take full account of the importance of families to children in the healthcare setting and recognize that child-friendly health care needs to encompass the diversity of circumstances in which children need health care and how it is provided must be appropriate to the child's stage of development, understanding, and needs.

The legal issue of consent

In Ireland, Section 23 of the Non-Fatal Offences against the Person Act 1997 provides that a person aged more than 16 years may give consent to 'surgical, medical or dental' treatment. It also provides that where a minor has given effective consent to treatment, it will not be necessary to obtain consent from their parent or guardian. Section 23 does not set out the position regarding children under 16 years, or make provision for the child's refusal of treatment.

In the United Kingdom, the House of Lords established the legal position of children under the age of 16 in 1986 in the Gillick case (*Gillick v West Norfolk and Wisbech AHA* [1986] AC 112). Mrs Gillick, the mother of five teenage daughters, complained that it would be unlawful for contraception advice and services to be provided to her daughters without her consent. The House of Lords disagreed, noting that a child under 16 years did not lack capacity by virtue of age alone, but acquired it, according to Lord Scarman, when the child 'reaches a sufficient understanding and intelligence to be capable of making up his own mind on the matter requiring decision'. Flowing from this, the key question is what must be understood by a child in order to achieve 'Gillick competence'. According to Lord Scarman (189):

> It is not enough that [the child] should understand the nature of the advice which is being given: she must also have a sufficient maturity to understand what is involved.

Although the standard is clearly very high (Herring and Gilmore 2011), the *Gillick* judgment was an important recognition of adolescent autonomy. Its principles have 'general application to all forms of medical treatment and assistance' (Fortin 2009: 147). Although *Gillick* recognizes the capacity of children under 16 years to consent to their own medical treatment, it does not presume that children under 16 years have this capacity; rather, the individual child must first prove it to the health professional involved (Fortin 2009). *Gillick* did not set out the precise test to be followed when determining the child's capacity to consent to the treatment in question based on the child's apparent understanding. This means that the child's capacity is to be determined by health professionals who may have their own views, attitudes, and perspectives on the child's capacity in this context (see BMA 2009).

Refusing medical treatment

Legal systems treat children who want to refuse medical treatment differently. In England and Wales, for example, the courts have developed the law in a way that acknowledges the capacity of children to refuse medical treatment while also protecting them from what might be considered more dangerous choices, such as when the treatment being refused is life-saving (Fortin 2009). This test has been developed in cases like *Re R (A Minor) (Wardship: Medical Treatment)* ([1992] Fam 11) to require that the child not only understands the nature of the proposed treatment but also that he or she fully understands and appreciates the consequences of both the treatment and the anticipated consequences of a failure to treat. The result is that the law requires much higher levels of competence from uncooperative adolescents than adults, and this is justified on the basis that they receive the medical treatment deemed essential to safeguard their health (Fortin 2009).

In Ireland, by contrast, the capacity of a child to refuse medical treatment – whether life-saving or not – has not yet arisen in the courts. Here, the family enjoys a protected status under the Irish Constitution (e.g. Articles 41.1 and 41.2). Article 42 of the Constitution outlines the State's duty to respect the parent–child relationship providing that the State will interfere in the family *only* in exceptional cases where there has been parental failure of a physical or moral kind. These provisions were found to apply to the healthcare setting in the case of *North Western Health Board v HW and CW* ([2001] 3 IR 622), where parents refused to consent to the PKU test (commonly known as the 'heelprick' test) being carried out on their child because they did not agree with puncturing the child's blood vessel. The Supreme Court considered that although perhaps an irrational decision, it was one that the parents were entitled to take within the autonomy of the family. Here, Justice Denham (725) explained that:

> [T]he test involves the weighing of all the circumstances, including parental responsibility, parental decisions, the child's personal rights, and the rights of all persons involved with and in the family, to determine in these circumstances what is in the best interests of the child.

In the circumstances, the refusal of the PKU test did not place the child at risk and no interference with the parents' rights was justified. There have been few other cases in which the courts have reached a similar conclusion. In a rare case, in 2004, for example, the High Court held that refusal of a blood transfusion by parents who were Jehovah's Witnesses did constitute 'exceptional' circumstances and permitted the hospital to provide the treatment to the child even though the parents refused (*The Irish Times*, 6 August 2004; the decision of Abbott J was not reported and the parties were not publicly identified).

Activity

- How does the legal framework in your country guide decision-making in the areas highlighted above? Consider (i) parents' refusal to consent to a minor procedure like the PKU test, and (ii) parents' refusal to consent to a more major procedure like a blood transfusion.
- With a group of peers, debate the ethical implications of each case with reference to the moral principles of beneficence and non-maleficence.

Parents' right to information

Jurisdictions also differ regarding who is entitled to receive information as to a child's medical treatment. In jurisdictions like England and Wales, the right to information generally follows the law on the capacity to consent, meaning that children who are considered capable of consenting to medical treatment have the right to object to others having access to their medical records. In Ireland, the matter is again complicated by the Constitution. For instance, the case of *McK v The Information Commissioner* ([2004] IEHC 4) recognized that parents have a general right to access their child's medical records even when their child is old enough to consent. This is based on the presumption that parents will act in the best interests of their child and as a result a parent is entitled to information about a child's medical care so that he or she can make appropriate decisions for the child as their guardian. Irish law thus suggests that parents have a broad if not unlimited right to remain involved in their child's healthcare decision-making even where the child has reached the age of consent to medical treatment. Although children's autonomy, especially for those children considered sufficiently mature, is a stronger element of the legal framework in England and Wales, nurses must always be prepared to negotiate between a child's desire for confidentiality and a parent's right to information. Such situations present ethical if not legal dilemmas. For example, the Medical Council of Ireland's (2009: 41) Guide to Professional Conduct and Ethics advises that when confronted by a patient under 16 who seeks to take a healthcare decision without the knowledge of consent of their parents: 'You should encourage the patient to involve their parents in the decision, bearing in mind your paramount responsibility to act in the patient's best interests'. It is clear, therefore, that the paramount ethical responsibility lies with protecting the child's interests. Open communication and consultation with children and with their parents (separately) is clearly the ideal way to avoid any formal clash between parents and their children.

Reflection point

What are the legal rules governing a parent's access to medical records where the child does not consent?

If a parent asked you for the medical records of his or her child, knowing that the child (and/or legal guardian, if applicable) were opposed to this, how would you deal with the situation?

Reflect on how you would resolve the ethical considerations of sharing a child's medical information with his or her parent where the child strongly objects.

Refusing medical treatment

Irish law is silent on whether children over 16 years (who may consent to medical treatment) have the right to refuse such treatment. The Irish courts have yet to consider this matter, although the English courts have held that children under 18 are not entitled to refuse medical treatment (see *Re R. (A Minor)* [1991] 4 All E.R. 177 and *Re W. (A Minor)* [1992] 4 All E.R. 627). Therefore, if a child or young person under the age of 18 refuses treatment, a parent or guardian may override the child's wishes and give a legally binding consent on his or her behalf. If the parent declines to do this, the court has ultimate authority to give consent on behalf of the child if it considers that the treatment in question is in the child's interests. It is more difficult to predict what an Irish court would do, although it is clear, given the constitutional position, that the position of the parents will be pivotal.

Activity

How would you respond if a child objected to having medical treatment but the parent wanted the child to have it?

Respecting the child's physical integrity

In law and ethics, consent to medical treatment is bound up with respect for physical integrity. Even very young children have strong views on whether they wish to have a procedure or treatment and their responses to proposed procedures may range from wiling agreement to full-scale rejection. The fact that a parent will normally have formal legal authority to consent on their child's behalf does not render the child's consent irrelevant (Kilkelly and Donnelly 2010). For example, using physical means to force a reluctant child to comply with a medical procedure may breach the child's rights regardless of whether the parent has consented to the treatment.

Vignette   Physical restraint: Robbie's case

Robbie, who is 5 years old, is experiencing pain following an appendectomy. Efforts to manage Robbie's pain with oral paracetamol have been unsuccessful because he has vomited the medication each time it has been administered. Following discussion with his parents, it was decided to prescribe a paracetamol suppository for rectal administration. When the nurse attempted to insert the suppository, Robbie immediately became upset and physically fought off the nurse by kicking her. His parents, whose priority was that Robbie would not be in pain, held him down despite his resistance. The nurse was then able to administer the suppository. Robbie's mum then took him into her arms and cuddled him while he sobbed quietly.

Activity

Before reading an analysis of Robbie's case below, consider the following questions:

- Is the use of force on Robbie justified based on the principle of acting in his 'best interests'?
- What are Robbie's rights in this situation, and have his rights been breached?
- What are the ethical challenges of this case?

(Address the latter question within the moral framework of Beauchamp and Childress (2009) on 'what ought to be' based on the principles of beneficence, non-maleficence, autonomy, justice, veracity, and fidelity.)

In Robbie's case, both the nurse and parents seemed to work in his 'best interests' to alleviate his pain. However, Robbie was resisting this procedure indicating his lack of consent. Although no formal legal consent was required from Robbie, the use of force is a breach of his rights to dignity and bodily integrity. Robbie's case could be viewed as contravening the ethical principle of beneficence and non-maleficence. It is possible that Robbie's experience could leave him fearful of communicating about pain to healthcare professionals again and may leave him fearful of subsequent hospitalization or future encounters with nurses.

Robbie's case has implications for the exchange of relevant information. Children need to be informed about forthcoming procedures including what they entail, their purpose, hoped-for benefits, and what they are likely to experience.

A principal concern of children when undergoing procedures is whether these will hurt. The ethical principle of veracity requires that children be told the truth about what to expect. Yet, children often undergo medical procedures with little or no information about what is involved.

Children's experiences

> I felt awfully nervous the first time, it hurt real bad . . . I did it because what they did was so strange, that I didn't know at all how it was supposed to be done and how much it was going to hurt (lumbar puncture). (Pölkki et al. 1999: 24)
>
> [I thought] they were going to cut open my belly and stick their hand up and up and take out my tonsils, which was noted by his mother, frightened the life out of him. (Buckley and Savage 2010: 2883)

Children do not wish to be placated in terms of being 'very good' during a procedure without knowing what is happening to them. Telling children that a procedure will be 'okay' and 'nothing to worry about' does little to address the principle of veracity. Children's consent to procedures can be gained in a cooperative way by providing them with information and having them actively involved.

Child perspective

> 'I put the sleeping ointment on my arm . . . and I have the drawing with me'. When the children understood the 'successful' result of the EMLA ointment, they often confirmed: 'It was like you said . . . a little pressure . . . and no stabbing . . . almost no pressure either'. (Wennstrom et al. 2008: 102)

According to Jaaniste et al. (2007), communicating about healthcare procedures to a child should not be viewed as a discreet, unidirectional intervention, but rather as a transactional social process involving continuing interactions with the child. Therefore, when informing children about a procedure, opportunities to explore their views and related questions need to be built into the communication process.

Children's right to information

In law, generally, a patient has a legal entitlement to reasonable information about the risks involved in treatment, and whether the consent is being given by the child or by a parent on their child's behalf, the same general level of information should be provided. Moreover, even if a child does not have the capacity to consent under the law, they are nonetheless entitled to information as to their treatment.

In certain circumstances, like Sarah's case, the nurse will have to cope with a child who wants information and the parent who does not want them to have it.

Vignette   Parents as information gatekeepers: Sarah's case

Sarah has been HIV-infected since birth. Sarah's HIV-infected mother has never wanted Sarah to be informed about her diagnosis or why she was taking medication other than telling her that she needed medication 'to keep her blood clean'. Over the years, Sarah's mother has made it very clear that healthcare professionals are not to disclose any information to Sarah about having HIV. When Sarah was 13 years old, healthcare professionals broached the subject of disclosure with her mother but she remained adamant that her daughter was not to be informed about being HIV-infected. During a clinic consultation one day when Sarah was on her own with a nurse, she asked: 'What exactly is wrong with my blood'?

Activity

Similar to Sarah's case, Klitzman et al. (2008) draw attention to questions that may be confronted in this situation:

- Does Sarah have a right to know her diagnosis and the nature of HIV infection?
- Does Sarah's mother have the right to withhold information from her?
- What should Sarah be told now about her blood condition?
- What are the benefits and risks of addressing or not addressing Sarah's question?
- What are the legal implications of informing Sarah about her diagnosis against her mother's wishes?

Before reading an analysis of Sarah's case below, consider your response to each of the questions posed by Klitzman et al. (2008).

In the absence of legal guidance on whether and what information to disclose to children, nurses and other healthcare professionals must take difficult ethical decisions. An analysis of ethical issues concerning disclosure of HIV infection to children and adolescents (Klitzman et al. 2008) highlights the need to weigh up the principles of autonomy, beneficence, non-maleficence, and justice. Applied to Sarah's case, arguments for disclosure include her right to know what is wrong with her blood (autonomy), that this information will increase her awareness of the need for safe practices once sexually active (beneficence), avoiding deception of the child (maleficence), and consideration of public health relating to safe sexual practices to avoid spread of HIV (justice). Arguments against disclosure include the mother's right to decide about disclosure and that is privileged over healthcare professionals' wishes. While non-disclosure may protect the child from the burden associated with knowing the stigmatizing and life-threatening nature of HIV (beneficience), disclosure may impose considerable psychological burden on the child (maleficience).

Open communication policies work best for children and their families in the case of HIV (Gerson *et al.* 2001; Lesch *et al.* 2007; Vaz *et al.* 2010) and other illnesses such as cancer (Scott *et al.* 2003; Clarke *et al.* 2005). This is reflective of a children's rights approach. Open communication needs to be negotiated with parents and they may need to be supported in this process over time such that information be paced, taking account of the child's age and maturity. As children get older, they can be expected to handle more complex information. However, there are no definitive chronological ages that represent the best time points for communicating with children about their health. Children of similar ages can vary considerably in terms of maturity and readiness to engage in discussions about their health. It cannot be assumed that children do not think about or question their health from a young age. For example, young children with chronic illnesses may begin to ask questions when they notice apparent differences between themselves and their siblings or school peers such as taking regular medication. Supporting the role of parents is paramount because most communication with children about their health and related illnesses is likely to take place in the home.

Parent perspective

I don't know what to say to her when she asks me. I have to think quick, and then I might be giving her the wrong answer. She knows some people die of cancer, some people live longer, some people need less treatment, some people need more treatment, it's just some people get more poorly than others. She won't accept that, she thinks because she's got cancer she's not going to live to be an old lady and have a family of her own. (Young *et al.* 2002: 1842)

If parents consistently evade a child's questioning or adopt a closed communication strategy concerning their health, children may question nurses. In Sarah's case, while the nurse may have previously mulled over the legal and ethical implications of informing Sarah about her HIV infection against her mother's wishes, she is now challenged to respond 'on the spot' to Sarah's questioning. In this situation, an experienced nurse with a wealth of case knowledge and who knows Sarah and her mother over time is likely to handle this situation by responding gently with a probing question: 'What do you think is wrong with your blood?' This question may help to open the conversation and glean Sarah's understanding of her health status. From here, the nurse can further explore what information Sarah would like to have about her health. The decision about directly answering Sarah's question during the conversation remains an ethical one, weighing up the pros and cons. Because of the mother's request not to inform Sarah about being HIV-infected, the nurse may feel obliged not to directly answer Sarah's question. However, the use of tactful probing questions could provide Sarah with an opportunity to express her views and concerns. This conversation could then lead to an agreement that the nurse follows up on Sarah's concerns by negotiating the support of her mother to allow Sarah to learn about her health. In applying the ethical principle of fidelity, the nurse must now keep this agreement. The challenge of negotiating with Sarah's mother about disclosing information to her child remains. In this case, a plan for open communication could be put in place and this would need to be paralleled with professional support.

Reflection point

Consider a clinical situation that you have encountered in which a parent has clearly communicated that they do not want their child to be given information about their diagnosis or related treatment, even if the child asks for this information.

- How did you handle this situation at the time?
- What legal and ethical knowledge informed your thoughts on how best to handle this situation?
- If you encountered this situation again, would you handle it any differently and why?

The importance of children's participation

Article 12 of the United Nations Convention on the Rights of the Child provides that every child capable of forming a view has the right to express that view and have it taken into account in all matters affecting him or her. The United Nations Committee on the Rights of the Child (2009) noted that children's participation in healthcare decision-making depends on children being provided with sufficient information, conveyed in an accessible form. The Committee recommended that where a child can demonstrate capacity to express an informed view on her or his treatment, this view must be given due weight. The child's right to have a say and be involved in decisions made about them is relevant to all children in the healthcare setting, regardless of age. This concept of participation is as central to good nursing practice as it is to a children's rights approach. For clinical situations in which no clear legal advice is available, nurses should consider applying the Code of Practice developed by Alderson and Montgomery (1996) as a framework for communicating with children. It involves four levels of participation:

1. taking part in exchange of relevant information;
2. sharing in decision-making by expressing a view;

3. influencing a decision by consenting or withholding consent to proposed treatment if competent to do so, subject to the supervisory role of the courts;
4. exercising autonomy as a main decision-maker, subject to specific legal limitations.

Vignette   Decision-making: Karl's case

Karl, who is 12 years old, has cystic fibrosis. Over the past year he has been having recurrent chest infections and has had difficulty maintaining his weight. Healthcare professionals and Karl's parents have repeatedly reinforced his need to eat more. Despite Karl's best efforts, he continued to lose weight. It was decided to tube feed Karl. In the past, Karl had always been involved in discussions about his health and now refused to be tube fed. He was advised by his parents and healthcare professionals that this was not a matter up for choice. Karl was not happy with the decision and said that even if a tube was inserted, he would pull it out.

Activity

Having read through Karl's case and commentary, consider how you would communicate with Karl and his parents to resolve their differences regarding tube feeding. You could try this activity with peers using role-play.

- What aspects of this communication may be particularly challenging for you?
- What tensions need to be addressed between the rights of Karl and his parents?

Consider the latter question within the context of the rights of the child under the Convention on the Rights of the Child (United Nations 1989).

These levels of participation are subject to a child's level of competence and specific legal limitations (Alderson and Montgomery 1996). Earlier in this chapter, we cited the *Gillick* case to illustrate the replacement of the aged-based legal limitation on children less than 16 years consenting to treatment with an individual-based assessment of a child's maturity and intellectual ability. However, in the case of a child refusing to consent to treatment, as in Karl's case, the age-based legal limitation applies (see 'Refusing consent to medical treatment').

Karl's case is more complex than the cases of Robbie and Sarah because it explicitly illustrates a child's refusal of treatment that is potentially life-saving. The challenge for healthcare professionals is to communicate with Karl in ways that gain his cooperation because even if his parents legally consent to tube feeding, Karl could purposively pull out the tube. A starting point might be to establish why Karl is refusing to be tube fed. He may be concerned about body image because of marks the tube may leave on his skin; he may be worried about what peers will think if they notice a tube under his T-shirt. Unlike his parents and healthcare professionals, Karl's priorities for being healthy may not concern weight gain to prevent chest infections.

Similar to evidence from children with cystic fibrosis (Savage and Callery 2005, 2007), Karl's principal concern may be whether he has energy to play and do the things he likes to do every day. Consequently, it could be explained to Karl that tube feeding will provide him with more energy to play football. Providing information relevant to the 'here and now' and that directly impacts on children's personal lives is more meaningful to them than information that focuses on medical goals and future health (Savage and Callery 2005, 2007).

In the event that a child continues to refuse a treatment, it is recommended that where possible the treatment be postponed to allow the child time to reconsider (Alderson and Montgomery 1996). Postponing treatment may allow children time to reflect on the situation and to ask further questions of relevance to them. Giving children time, if possible, demonstrates to them that they are being listened to. When children are informed about their condition and consulted on decisions that affect them, they are more willing to cooperate with treatments (Franklin and Sloper 2005). However, children often want their parents to retain formal responsibility for decisions relating to their health. The ideal position would be that most healthcare decisions be taken by parents and children together, without artificial distinctions about who is legally responsible (Alderson and Montgomery 1996).

Conclusion

This chapter has attempted to identify and tease out the legal and ethical implications of communicating with children and their parents. Although the law provides only a loose framework for involving children in healthcare decision-making, it nonetheless sets important parameters about the right of parents to be involved and the right of children to have their rights respected. The aims of the exemplars and reflective exercises were to highlight how clinical challenges in this area might be met, and to illustrate the coherence between best practice and the legal and ethical framework in relation to nurses' communication with children and their patients.

Key messages

- The law provides a framework, which, together with ethical practice, offers broad principles to guide nurses in their communication with children.
- Even if children are not legally entitled to consent, regard must be had to their right to physical integrity, and their right to participate in the decision-making process around their health.
- In all cases, nurses should be sensitive to the particular needs and circumstances of children and of their parents.

References

Alderson, P. and Montgomery, J. (1996) *Health Care Choices: Making Decisions with Children.* London: Institute for Public Policy Research.

Beauchamp, T.L. and Childress, J.F. (2009) *Principles of Biomedical Ethics*, 6th edn. New York: Oxford University Press.

British Medical Association (BMA) (2009) *Consent Tool Kit*, 5th edn. London: BMA.

Buckley, A. and Savage, E. (2010) Preoperative information needs of children undergoing tonsillectomy, *Journal of Clinical Nursing*, 19: 2879–87.

Clarke, S.-A., Davies, H., Jenney, M., Glaser, A. and Eiser, C. (2005) Parental communication and children's behaviour following diagnosis of childhood leukaemia, *Psycho-Oncology*, 14(4): 274–81.

Donnelly, M. (2002) *Consent: Bridging the Gap Between Doctor and Patient.* Cork: Cork University Press.

Fortin, J. (2009) *Children's Rights and the Developing Law*, 3rd edn. Cambridge: Cambridge University Press.

Franklin, A. and Sloper, P. (2005) Listening and responding? Children's participation in health care within England, *International Journal of Children's Rights*, 13(1/2): 11–29.

Gerson, A.C., Joyner, M., Fosarelli, P., Butz, A., Wissow, L., Lee, S. *et al.* (2001) Disclosure of HIV diagnosis to children: when, where, why and how, *Journal of Pediatric Health Care*, 15(4): 161–7.

Herring, J. and Gilmore, S. (2011) No is the hardest word: consent and children's autonomy, *Child and Family Law Quarterly*, 3–31.

Jaaniste, T., Hayes, B. and von Baeyer, C.L. (2007) Providing children with information about forthcoming medical procedures: a review and synthesis, *Clinical Psychology: Science and Practice*, 14(2): 124–43.

Kilkelly, U. and Donnelly, M. (2007) *The Child's Right to be Heard in the Healthcare Setting: Perspectives of Children, Parents and Healthcare Professionals.* Dublin: Office of the Minister for Children.

Kilkelly, U. and Donnelly, M. (2010) Participation in healthcare: the views and experiences of children and young people, *International Journal of Children's Rights*, 19: 1–25.

Klitzman, R., Marhefka, S., Mellins, C. and Wiener, L. (2008) Ethical issues concerning disclosure of HIV diagnoses to perinatally infected children and adolescents, *Journal of Clinical Ethics*, 19(1): 31–42.

Lesch, A., Swartz, L., Kagee, A., Moodley, K., Zafaar, Z., Myer, L. *et al.* (2007) Pediatric HIV/AIDS disclosure: towards a development and process-oriented approach, *AIDS Care*, 19(6): 811–16.

Medical Council of Ireland (2009) *Guide to Professional Conduct and Ethics*, 7th edn. Dublin: Medical Council of Ireland.

Pölkki, T., Pietilä, A.M. and Rissanen, L. (1999) Pain in children: qualitative research of Finnish school-aged children's experiences of pain in hospital, *International Journal of Nursing Practice*, 5: 21–8.

Savage, E. and Callery, P. (2005) Weight and energy: parents' and children's perspectives on managing cystic fibrosis diet, *Archives of Disease in Childhood*, 90(3): 249–52.

Savage, E. and Callery, P. (2007) Clinic consultations with children and parents on the dietary management of cystic fibrosis, *Social Science and Medicine*, 64(2): 363–74.

Scott, J.T., Prictor, M., Harmsen, M., Broom, A., Entwistle, V.A., Sowden, A.J. *et al.* (2003) Interventions for improving communication with children and adolescents about a family member's cancer, *Cochrane Database of Systematic Reviews*, Issue 4. Art. No. CD004511.

United Nations (1989) *Convention on the Rights of the Child*. Geneva: United Nations.

United Nations Committee on the Rights of the Child (2009) *The Child's Right to be Heard*, General Comment No. 12, CRC/GC/2009/12.

Vaz, L., Eng, E., Maman, S., Tshikandu, T. and Behets, F. (2010) Telling children they have HIV: lessons learned from findings of a qualitative study in sub-Saharan Africa, *AIDS Patient Care and STDs*, 24(4): 247–56.

Wennstrom, B., Hallberg, L.R.M. and Bergh, I. (2008) Use of peri-operative dialogues with children undergoing day surgery, *Journal of Advanced Nursing*, 62(1): 96–106.

Young, B., Dixon-Woods, M., Findlay, M. and Heney, D. (2002) Parenting in crisis: conceptualising mothers of children with cancer, *Social Science and Medicine*, 55: 1835–47.

Communicating with children and young people in research

Joan Livesley and Tony Long

Research with children and young people is both necessary and desirable. Despite a prevailing culture that focuses on protecting children and young people from perceived potential harm, often to the extent that they are excluded from participation in research, it is both possible and essential to allow and facilitate children's and young people's involvement in research that affects them. In this chapter, we consider first the roles that children and young people might play in research studies and why these might give cause for concern. We discuss the need to strike a balance between protective exclusion and facilitated inclusion. We move on to the means to enable children's and young people's contributions and the skills needed by the researcher to facilitate participation by all those who wish to make a contribution.

Learning outcomes

By the end of this chapter you should be able to:

1. Appreciate the nature of 'voice' in research with children and young people
2. Identify some problems in eliciting children's voice
3. Extend the personal repertoire of techniques to enhance communication with children and young people in research

---

Why should we worry about communicating with children in research?

There are three possible roles that children and young people might undertake in association with research:

1. They may be participants (subjects) in research studies. This is the most likely way in which they will play a part.

2. They may enhance the research process by advising researchers on study design, formulation of information sheets, and evaluating the process and outcomes of a study.
3. They also may take a more active role, perhaps collecting data from other children and young people.

Each role requires careful thought on the part of the researcher to ensure that the research is conducted as rigorously and effectively as possible and that young participants (in whatever role) are not exploited or harmed. The risks of exploitation and harm are often heightened when researching sensitive issues with vulnerable groups. Research with children and young people is essential both to improve specific services for them and to ensure that they are not excluded from possible benefits from research.

Despite the reservations held by many adults (we will address these shortly), children and young people have things to say and they want to be heard. They often want to make a difference – for other children if not for themselves. It is important not to exclude the most vulnerable children or to avoid the most difficult topics, since these may be the populations and issues that require the most attention.

For the researcher, this translates into a number of concerns that arise from allowing and encouraging children and young people to participate in research while simultaneously protecting them from being harmed by the study. It is a matter of striking a balance between inclusion and exclusion (Figure 11.1). This means that researchers must: (1) avoid exploitation (but who decides when it becomes exploitation?); (2) protect from danger (but allow some risks and avoid exclusion); and (3) hear the voice (but whose voice will be heard?).

It is incumbent on researchers to manage these concerns by ensuring that:

- children that participate are aware of their role and understand the researcher's expectations of them;
- the researcher is able to hear what the children want to say;
- children's preferences, concerns, and responses can be addressed on their terms.

Activity

Throughout this chapter we use a number of key concepts, including:

Agency	Inclusion
Children's voice	Participation
Competence	Protection
Gatekeeper	Proxy
Generation	Social agents

Take some time to read around these terms and write down your own definition for each. As you continue to read through the chapter, check your understanding of the terms.

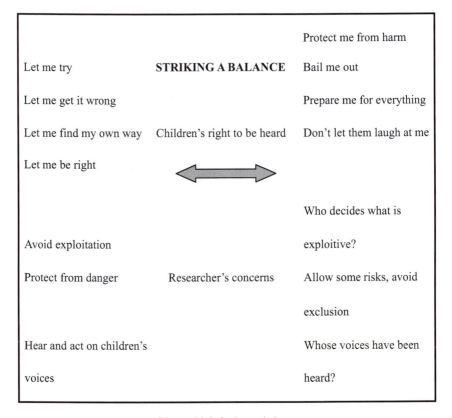

Figure 11.1 Striking a balance

Eliciting children's voices

Positioning children and young people

The last 30 years have seen a tremendous upsurge in scholarly interest and publications related to concepts of childhood and what it means to be a child. Unlike other marginalized members of society, children have relied on adult advocates to advance their best interests and develop structures that enable their voices to be heard. As Hendrick (1992: 4) noted:

> Unlike women, black people, and the working class, children are not in a position either to write their own history, or to ask awkward questions of those who exercise power and control over them. Nor do they have a political movement to raise public consciousness of their condition and their grievances.

Historically, and to a large degree still today, the dominant assumption has been that children cannot speak for themselves or that, when they do, their accounts lack veracity (Fivush 2002; Vrij 2002). In spite of the growing acceptance of children as social agents, it seems that, for some, the validity of children's voices is still questionable (Oates 2007). At a time when there is a growing emphasis on participating with children and taking their views seriously, there is a growing social panic and increasing public anxiety around children.

In spite of the growing acceptance of children as social agents – defined by John (2003) as individuals who influence and shape their own world – and the right of children to be involved in matters that impact on their lives, research activity with children has been subject to increasing control and governance (Danby and Farrell 2004). Some progress has been made and advocacy groups such as INVOLVE and Participation Works, together with the appointment of a Children's Commissioner for England and an Ombudsman for Children in Ireland, have provided further impetus in driving forward children's right to be heard and have their views acted on. A discernible tension is evident between the view of children as active participants in their own social situations and the traditional construction of children as 'pre-competent or developing in competence' (Danby and Farrell 2004: 36). Still, children are most often positioned as the property of their parents.

The power of the proxy voice: silencing children

The problem with this deeply entrenched view of children as being the property of their parents, incompetent and unable to speak for themselves, is that others must always speak for them. These 'others' may not represent accurately the views and values that children hold. This matters because most research that is undertaken about children is based on responses from adults (parents, teachers, and professionals) and not with the children themselves. The result is that children's voices are not heard. Instead, a proxy report is acquired – the proxy (adult) voice.

Activity

Aldridge and Wood (1997) sought to reconcile their analysis of transcriptions from interviews with children who had been abused with findings from studies of non-clinical samples of children. Findings from other research suggested that children who met standard developmental norms could 'spontaneously comment on the intentions, feelings and desires experienced by themselves and others,' and 'from the age of 36 months can accurately identify situations that elicit simple emotional reactions like happiness, sadness, anger and fear' (p. 1222). Their own analysis of transcripts from videotaped forensic interviews with children was that some children seemed to be unable or unwilling to discuss feelings regarding their personal experience of abuse.

Take a few minutes to think of the reasons for this contradiction. Think about the proxy voice and views of children's ability.

Aldridge and Wood suggested that the difference in findings between their work and that of other researchers was due an over-reliance on maternal reporting of children's ability and the use of researcher emotional cue strategies. This, they argued, led to an over-estimation of children's ability.

The right of children to express their views

The view of children as active social agents is enshrined in the United Nations (1989) Convention on the Rights of the Child, in particular Article 12 (children's views should be given due weight in accordance with their age and maturity) and Article 13 (the right to freedom of expression). While in Ireland 'there is currently no national strategy or policy document dedicated to the health of children, setting out the rights to which children are entitled, and treatment to which they can expect in hospital and community health care settings and the measures to be implemented to ensure goals and standards are met' (Kilkelly 2008: 408), in the UK the current policy directing the care of children in hospital reflects these rights of children (Department of Health 2004). A central tenet of this policy is that all children, regardless of their ability, age, ethnic background or social class, have the right to express their views on what happens to them and to have those views taken seriously by adults delivering services. However, these rights are conditional and are tempered by the capacity of children, responsibilities and rights of parents, and national legislation. In this context, participation and involvement are substantial conceptual tools to help nurses and researchers to work with children to enable their participation and decision-making activities.

Activity

Look a little further. Many groups exist to further respect for children's rights. For examples, see the Children's Rights Alliance for England and Ireland at http://www.crae.org.uk/rights/uncrc.html and http://www.childrensrights.ie/, respectively, and the World Health Organization's Self Evaluation Model and Tool on the Respect for Children's Rights in Hospital at http://www.who.int/pmnch/topics/child/200901_childrights/en/index.html

Learning a new meaning of 'voice'

It is important for researchers to challenge the often taken-for-granted assumption that adults are competent commentators on children's experiences. Part of this is coming to understand that being heard is a not a one-dimensional concept relating only to that which is spoken or verbally expressed. Children express themselves in much more than what they say. Silences, smiles, and other elements of non-verbal communication are an equally important part of their efforts to convey their views and wishes to others.

Activity

In 2011, a mother of twin boys posted a stunning example of this on the Internet. These toddlers hold what is clearly a lengthy conversation – with never a word spoken. Watch the exchange at http://www.twinmamarama.com/twinconversation

- What is it that makes it seem that the toddlers are engaging in a conversation?
- Is it what they say?
- Is there something else?

Christensen (2004) noted that adults sometimes make the mistake of using mechanisms that are familiar to adults in structuring adult–child relations rather than taking the time to observe children and identify the preferred mechanisms that individual children use to communicate. Researchers need to adopt a raft of creative methods to enable the inclusive participation of children and to enable their contribution in research studies. Children – especially younger children – need to be helped to use a variety of means to express their voice.

Activity

Watch the video posted on YouTube at http://www.youtube.com/watch?v=-fVDGu82FeQ. Consider the following questions and write down you answers:

- What was the young boy trying to communicate?
- Do you share his concerns? Are they reasonable?
- How would you describe his feelings at this time?
- Are his preferences, concerns, and responses being addressed?
- Why do adults find this recording so amusing?
- What would you have done had you been a researcher present during this exchange?

For their part, researchers need to learn how to 'read' children's responses and to allow children to take the lead in the exchange. A similar situation exists in research with young people. Most teenagers are perfectly able to express their views but will often choose to do so in ways that are familiar and meaningful to them. In such cases, the use of text messaging, social networking or flip video recording may be the preferred means of communication. In particular, SMS text messaging has been reported as an effective method for communication in research studies (Anhøj and Møldrup 2004; Fry and Neff 2009; Bexelius *et al.* 2010). In all cases, the onus must fall on researchers to facilitate effective communication. They must do the work – not the children.

Enabling children's contributions

A number of communication problems are commonly encountered in research with children and young people. These begin before the study starts and continue to the end of the study. Here we deal with two particular problems: gaining access and ensuring informed consent. We consider the partial usefulness of a particular framework for interviewing children and use authentic research examples to investigate means to support children's participation in research.

Gaining access

While children's competence and capacity to understand is often greater than expected and their participation in some countries is considered unremarkable (Hart 1992), in other countries, such as Ireland and the UK, mechanisms and acceptance of children's involvement in research is less well-established and in need of further development (Hill *et al.* 2004; Alderson 2007; Coyne 2010). Although there has been some reported progress in the inclusion of children in matters that affect their lives (Murray and Hallett 2000; Coyne 2010), progress in health and youth justice services has been considerably slower (Carnevale *et al.* 2008). Fuelled by scandals published widely in the media, such as the Royal Liverpool Children's Hospital Inquiry (Redfern 2001), the NHS in England and Wales has been subject to increasing regulation and control (Long and Johnson 2007). This has done little to ease the process of gaining access to children for the purpose of research (Stalker *et al.* 2004).

The ethical considerations concerned with access for research work with children are different because of the fundamental need to consider the power and generational issues inherent in child–adult and child–practitioner relations (Punch 2002). Of particular concern in this chapter are issues of consent and the provision of information to children and young people. The Research and Governance Framework for Health and Social Care (Department of Health 2005: 7) stated that:

> Care is needed when seeking consent from children and from vulnerable adults, such as those with mental health problems or learning difficulties. Arrangements must be made to ensure that relevant information is provided in appropriate written or pictorial form, and that the role and responsibilities of parents, carers or supporters are clearly explained and understood.

Coyne (2009) has challenged the current position by pointing out that most of the published arguments are wrongly concerned with issues of power between children and adults rather than focusing on children's rights. Drawing on the self-determination principle set out in the UNCRC (United Nations 1989), she argues that it is children who should be consulted first rather than seeking access to them through gatekeepers. The challenges in gaining access, and obtaining both parent and child consent, were highlighted in the ethical review of children's research in Ireland (Office of the Minister for Children and Youth Affairs 2010).

Providing information for child participants

Some researchers have made brave attempts to develop specific techniques, such as games, to help children understand what is proposed and their role in it, and to elicit their consent (Runeson *et al.* 2000; Bray 2007). Reading these articles will increase your understanding of the benefits and problems of such possibilities. In the activity below, we provide an example of including children in the design of a study – specifically, the design of information sheets for child participants.

Activity

Think about creating information leaflets. In a study undertaken by one of the authors, access was negotiated with a local after-school club to consult with children on the design of a logo for the study. The children were invited to participate in a logo design and title competition. They were told that the researcher wanted to find out about what it was like for children who were admitted to hospital. The after-school club staff supervised the children for an hour, during which they sat together and drew pictures of what came into their minds when they thought about children in hospital. The children worked together in a group, chatting, sharing ideas, and looking at each other's work. Collectively, they agreed on a title for the work, and at the end of the session the children voted for the winning logo.

- What were the key issues that were attended to by the researcher?
- What indicators are there that the children participated willingly?
- What might the benefits be for communication of involving other children in this way?

Learning from forensic interviews

Some qualitative researchers have focused a great deal of attention on the reliability of the analytical processes used to derive rigorous findings from research (Koch 1996; Long and Johnson 2000; Rolfe 2006). While this is laudable, there has been far less critical attention paid to the processes used to establish what has counted as the voice of participants or how their voice has been elicited. There is, however, a substantial body of evidence that has been used to validate the credibility of children's testimony in criminal courts.

The UK Home Office and Department of Health jointly published the Memorandum of Good Practice (updated in 2007). The purpose of the Memorandum was to assist practitioners who were undertaking forensic interviews with children to derive evidence admissible in criminal courts. The Memorandum introduced a four-phase framework for forensic interview work with children. The four phases are:

- establishing a rapport
- eliciting free narrative
- questioning
- closing.

This structured approach to interviewing children, particularly when children's disclosure of events is being sought, has been refined and researched in a number of contexts and a number of countries (USA, UK, and Israel). Early research has reported high levels of satisfaction among professionals using the framework to conduct forensic interviews with children, and notably for 'reducing the stress for the child witness and for improving the quality of the child's account' (Aldridge and Wood 1997: 8). The first three of these phases will be considered in detail here.

Establishing a rapport

While children have good memories of events they have experienced, they are not used to being asked for their account of them. Some children may think adults with whom they are dealing know more than they do. Others may be naturally reticent, shy, have verbal or communication impairments or be unable to engage in lengthy conversations (Aldridge and Wood 1998). The researcher's task is to develop a range of strategies that will play to the strengths of individual children rather than emphasize their weaknesses or their difference from others, and enable them to engage effectively. In other words, they must establish a rapport and a meaningful relationship.

Activity

Davis et al. (2008) studied the experience of disabled children and how they negotiated their own social worlds in the context of a special school. They reported that some teaching staff were resistant to the notion that the children with communication impairment could participate actively. A further difficulty related to the fieldworker's concerns about the expectations that both the children and the staff would have about his behaviour. In his words, he 'didn't have a clue how [he] was expected to behave ... and found it extremely difficult to understand if the children were happy with [his] presence in their class' (p. 221).

Over time he discovered that the children did not associate his role with that of other adults in the school, but that they still used his status as an adult to achieve their best interests. Not only could the children participate as required, but they could manipulate the situation to their advantage.

What lessons should we learn from this encounter for our own approaches to engaging children in research?

Eliciting free narrative accounts

According to the Memorandum, the free narrative phase of the interview is about listening to a child and encouraging him or her to 'provide in his or her own words and at his or her own pace an account of the relevant event(s)' (Home Office 2007: 17). The free narrative phase of the interview provides a means to elicit uncontaminated accounts from children. Strategies that are known to enable children during the free narrative phase include having supportive adults present at the time of the interview and using capability-relevant language. The use of supportive utterances, comments, and non-verbal affirmations such as nods are known further to mediate and support (to 'scaffold') children's efforts. There is an important balance to reach between giving children the time to express their views, repeating questions children did not respond to, and pressing them into giving the answer that they think is being sought.

Some researchers working with children have taken account of these concerns, and some have developed and reflected on a number of techniques used to engage with children of different ages effectively (Fraser *et al.* 2004; Lewis *et al.* 2004). Others have relied on specific methods such as drawing (Coates 2004), story-telling (Sutton *et al.* 2004), and theatrical techniques (Evans and Norman 2002). These strategies offer effective solutions for researchers attempting to realize the full potential of contributions from children, but they often rely on repeating the techniques with limited flexibility with each child. This means that, although creative, when used in isolation some methods could become self-limiting. A different approach is the mosaic technique, which involves using a range of strategies to prevent children from becoming bored or tired of more usual approaches taken by adults (Clark 2004). More recently still, attention has turned to consider the benefits of using art and craft techniques (Coad *et al.* 2009). A review of some of these reports reveals fascinating detail of children's responses and the positive outcomes that can be achieved.

Questioning children

When children offer a free narrative account, missing contextual detail and a lack of facts often limit the usefulness of what has been elicited. There is then the need for a questioning phase to probe, clarify, and check understanding. There is evidence that certain questioning techniques, such as providing contextual detail, can be used in direct work with children to enhance their memory correspondence (accuracy) and enable them to communicate more detail (Coulbourn Faller 2007).

Closed questions have a greater propensity to elicit inaccurate answers and the questioning phase of any interview is perhaps the most likely to render inaccurate testimony. For instance, there is a positive correlation between leading closed questions and erroneous answers (Bourg *et al.* 1999). In particular, tag questions are known to be particularly difficult to resist. A tag question is one in which a positive statement is followed by a negative, or a negative statement is followed by a positive; for instance, 'he is very nice, isn't he'. Along with the intonation used, the tag question can be highly suggestive and very likely to elicit the suggested answer, regardless of the accuracy of this. While negative tag questions are seldom used in day-to-day conversations, positive tag questions are more common and therefore more likely to be used by researchers.

Activity

This is a brief activity about tag questions. Listen to a conversation between two adults for a few minutes.

• How many tag questions are used.
• How often does the response coincide with the suggestion.

If you have a legitimate opportunity, repeat this with a conversation between an adult and a child.

Regardless of children's ability to remember, the dynamic nature of memory means that other influences can have either an enhancing or deleterious impact. However, there is some evidence that the longer it takes to communicate a free narrative, the greater the number of words used and the greater the amount of contextual detail added, the greater is the likelihood that the recall will be accurate (Pezdek and Hinz 2002). This underlines the need for researchers attempting to elicit children's views to remain mindful of the need for supportive and complementary methods that maximize children's strengths, rather than methods that demean, supplant or disadvantage children.

Supporting children and overcoming hurdles

Researchers ought to include children and young people in research rather than exclude them. This means that the most inclusive research will involve children with varying disabilities, special needs, and culturally diverse personal experiences. It is probable that inclusive researchers will encounter a number of significant hurdles. These hurdles are for the researchers to overcome and include the need to overcome adult explanations of the children's experiences that are different to their own, vocabulary impoverishment, limited linguistic capacity, nervousness, fear of reprisals, and the difficulty inherent in the expression of emotion. Taking an inclusive approach to children's participation is not easy, but several research examples should help to show both the problem and some solutions.

Overcoming adult explanations

One girl's mother explained why she thought that the pain specialist nurse was particularly important for children who had undergone complex surgery. To illustrate this, her mother offered an example relating to pain scores. She said 'It had gone down with a jump from a $2^1/_2$ to a 1'. However, the girl disagreed: 'No, from a 4 to $2^1/_2$'. This conversation between the girl and her mother continued until they came to an agreement that the exact detail did not matter. While not the case for all children, this girl showed that she was not willing to have her account misinterpreted.

Activity

- What was the outcome of the girl's attempt to assert her own version of her story?
- How had her mother reacted to her disagreement?
- Was this a positive contribution to the interview or did it damage the process?

This encounter provides evidence that children can and will challenge a parent's account when it differs from their own. In this case, the girl was allowed to negotiate with her mother (rather than be dismissed as incompetent). More importantly, their discussion promoted the opportunity for the girl to go on and explain how she interpreted the numbers on the pain ladder. The disagreement had provided the right conditions for her knowledge to emerge and be accepted as valid.

Overcoming linguistic inability

The example below illustrates the impact of linguistic ability and vocabulary on eliciting children's knowledge. It underlines the importance not only of having supportive adults but the role that supportive children can play, too. In a similar way to adults, some children are willing to intervene and support other children to enable them to give their account and express their thoughts and feelings.

Kasir, a 9-year-old boy, described by his foster parents as having learning difficulties and communication problems, presented a challenging research encounter. He appeared to be especially dependent on his foster parents and his sister to enable him to communicate. Although younger than him, Kasir's sister was familiar with helping him to settle down in new situations and in helping him to answer questions. While at first she tended to interrupt and answer questions for him, she responded positively to her foster mother's request to let him answer for himself if he could. However, she continued to sit with him and play with him throughout the interview. Being interviewed in the presence of his sister and foster parents seemed to help Kasir to cope with the situation. This meant that he was able to articulate and describe his feelings during his stay in hospital.

Although Kasir had communication impairments, he was reliant on language to communicate as he did not use augmentative aids. However, he was unable to give a free narrative account of his experience. Instead, he gave most of his account through short, single-word answers. Given this, it was appropriate to probe and question him so that his views could be included.

Activity

Can you identify the techniques used by the researcher to overcome the problem.

Researcher: Kasir, how long were you in hospital for'?
Kasir: Dunno.
Researcher: Kasir, did you sleep in hospital?
Kasir: Yes.
Researcher: Do you know how many nights you slept in hospital?
Kasir: One day.
Researcher: Where did you sleep?
Kasir: In a bed.

This excerpt illustrates that using Kasir's name helped him to know that the questions were aimed at him, and offering contextual information ('did you sleep in hospital?') helped him to relate something about his interpretation of his hospital experience.

Activity

Try again with this short extract:

Researcher: Kasir. What was it like in hospital?
Kasir: Boring.
Researcher: Boring, why was it boring?
Kasir: [Silence]
Researcher: Kasir. Why was it boring?
Kasir: I was watching telly all day because I had nothing to do.

Repeating the question for a second time was another successful strategy that helped him to communicate and share his knowledge that his time in hospital had been boring. Using several different interview techniques, the researcher helped Kasir to communicate his interpretation of being in hospital. Making sure that his sister was involved meant that he was supported.

Overcoming nervousness

Jim appeared to be very nervous about taking part in a study. In spite of this, the researcher had been able to build a rapport with him and to scaffold his account by talking to him about an earlier experience of attending an accident and emergency department. Simple questions were used to facilitate his free narrative.

Reflection point

Review the use of questions in the following exchange:

Researcher: Had you ever been to casualty or anything like that?
Jim: I've been to casualty because I have a scar here.
Researcher: You have what?
Jim: Have a scar here.
Researcher: Oh, how did you get that?
Jim: And I've got another one here; I went through a glass mirror.
Researcher: How did you do that?
Jim: Well, there were two beds like that, and a glass mirror across, and I was with two of my friends, two girls, one of them my cousin and the other was my mum's friend's daughter. She jumped across it, and then my cousin jumped across it, and I jumped across it and I fell through it [pretends to jump].
Researcher: Oh dear, what, right through it like that? [pretends to jump as Jim had].

Overcoming reticence and embarrassment

The importance of establishing a rapport and gaining children's trust is an essential element in research with children. Some children are reticent to talk about the nature of their problems. For instance, while Jim was especially animated when he told how he had been to the accident and emergency department following the failed attempt to jump across a mirror placed between two beds, he was much more reticent to talk about his circumcision.

Reflection point

Read the following brief extract:

Jim: I was circumcised.
Researcher: OK. And is that because you had a problem?
Jim: I think, I had a bit of a problem, and my mum said it would be cleaner.

- What indicators are there even in this short extract that Jim was embarrassed to talk about his operation?
- How would you proceed with the interview?

Jim's answer is evasive and he diverts the researcher to his mother for further clarification. He did not refer to the reasons for the need for his circumcision again. With hindsight, had the researcher used an open question rather than a closed question he might have done so – but it is difficult to know. Would pushing him further to talk about it have been productive (or appropriate)?

This is a common problem for researchers investigating anything that may be embarrassing to children. Similarly, Seb was reticent to talk about his hypospadias.

Reflection point

Again, consider the following extract:

Researcher: What was it Seb, why did you have to go to the doctor?
Seb: Err, I had to have an operation.
Researcher: OK. Do you want to tell me why or would you rather not? You don't have to.
Seb: Do you know, do you know why?
Researcher: I don't know, but I can find out. Do you want me to find out?
Seb: It's just a bit embarrassing. That's all I'm saying.
Researcher: That's absolutely fine. OK.

- What do you think about the researcher's approach in this exchange?
- Whose needs did she put first?
- Who was in charge of the encounter (and, in particular, in charge of how much was divulged)?
- How does this fit with what you read about children's rights and the researcher's responsibility?

Overcoming shyness

Sometimes, as with Kasir, it is not that children are reticent; it is that they do not have the capability to reveal their knowledge without additional support. In a similar way to Kasir, Kay was shy and very quiet. Because of this she needed an extensive range of support to enable her participation. With Kay, the researcher used a finger puppet, drawings, and story-telling techniques, and frequently read to her. All worked as effective strategies to earn her trust, enable her communication, and support her inclusion in the study.

Kay chose the finger puppet from the researcher's toy bag when they first met. They agreed to call the finger puppet Princess Finger (PF). Princess Finger became important not only in how Kay communicated with the researcher, but how she did so with other adults, including her parents. Using Princess Finger and combining this with story-telling techniques proved to be a very effective strategy in enabling Kay's communicative competence:

Researcher: So what was your operation for, Kay?
Kay: Ur.
Researcher: Shall I try like this ... once upon a time, a long time ago there was a little girl called Kay, and she came to the hospital for an operation. Her operation was to make something better.
Researcher [PF]: 'Do you know what you are making better?'
Kay: I had my wee done.

As already noted, eliciting the children's voices meant going beyond verbal communication. For Kay, non-verbal communication was sometimes her preferred way of telling the researcher what had happened. While she was sometimes reluctant to talk, she would respond to Princess Finger through a series of nods, headshakes, and shrugs. The snippet below includes Kay's non-verbal responses.

Researcher: Because you had your wee done. Is it better now?
Kay: [Silence]
Researcher [PF]: 'And Kay's got a tube in her tummy. What is the tube for?'
Kay: [Smiles]
Researcher [PF]: 'Do you know? '
Kay: [Shakes her head]
Researcher [PF]: 'You don't know what the tube is for?'
Kay: [Silence]

Conclusion

We have argued that there is a deeply entrenched view of children as being the property of their parents, incompetent and unable to speak for themselves. This matters because research regarding children's lives and experiences are often understood from a proxy (adult) voice. Yet, children's right to be heard and have their views taken seriously, not least in research, is enshrined in the United Nations (1989) Convention on the Rights of the Child. Key to children's participation is striking the right balance between children's right to be heard and the researcher's concerns regarding the children's need for protection from exploitation and harm. As children express themselves in many different ways, researchers need to make sure that they 'read' children's responses and allow the children to lead on exchanges. Researchers who take time to observe individual children's preferred communication strategies, mirror these, and establish a rapport and scaffold children's communicative competence stand to benefit a great deal.

Key messages

- Although children's ability is commonly denied or underestimated, children of all ages usually want to have their voice heard, and they have important things to say about situations and actions that affect them.
- Children express themselves in a variety of ways, and researchers need to use skill and concentration to recognize and understand these varied elements of communication in order to elicit valid data.
- The researcher's approach to engaging children in research, whether as participants, advisers, or co-researchers, is crucial. Techniques can be learned to help the researcher, particularly with regard to helping children with limited linguistic ability to make their contribution.

References

Alderson, P. (2007) Competent children? Minors' consent to health care treatment and research, *Social Science and Medicine*, 65: 2272–83.

Aldridge, M. and Wood, J. (1997) Talking about feelings: young children's ability to express emotions, *Child Abuse and Neglect*, 21(12): 1221–33.

Aldridge, M. and Wood, J. (1998) *Interviewing Children: A Guide for Child Care and Forensic Practitioners*. Chichester: Wiley.

Anhøj, J. and Møldrup, C. (2004) Feasibility of collecting diary data from asthma patients through mobile phones and SMS (short message service): response rate analysis and focus group evaluation from a pilot study, *Journal of Medical Internet Research*, 6(4): e42.

Bexelius, C., Lof, M., Sandin, S., Trolle Lagerross, Y., Forsum, E. and Litton, J. (2010) Measures of physical activity using cell phones: validation using criterion methods, *Journal of Medical Internet Research*, 12(1): e2.

Bourg, W., Broderick, R., Flagor, R., Meeks K.D., Lang, E.D. and Butler, J. (1999) *A Child Interviewer's Guidebook*. London: Sage.

Bray, L. (2007) Developing an activity to aid informed assent when interviewing children and young people, *Journal of Research in Nursing*, 12(5): 447–57.

Carnevale, F., Macdonald, M., Bluebond-Langner, M. and McKeever, P. (2008) Using participant observation in pediatric health care settings: ethical challenges and solutions, *Journal of Child Health Care*, 12(18): 18–32.

Christensen, P. (2004) Children's participation in ethnographic research: issues of power and representation, *Children and Society*, 18: 165–76.

Clark, A. (2004) The mosaic approach and research with young children, in V. Lewis, V. Kellet, C. Robinson, S. Fraser and S. Ding (eds) *The Reality of Research with Children and Young People*. London: Sage.

Coad, J., Plumridge, G. and Metcalfe, A. (2009) Involving children and young people in the development of art-based research tools, *Nurse Researcher*, 16(4): 56–64.

Coates, E. (2004) 'I forgot the sky!': children's stories contained within their drawings, in V. Lewis, V. Kellet, C. Robinson, S. Fraser and S. Ding (eds) *The Reality of Research with Children and Young People*. London: Sage.

Coulbourn Faller, K. (2007) Questioning techniques, in K. Coulbourn Faller (ed.) *Interviewing Children about Sexual Abuse: Controversies and Best Practice*. Oxford: Oxford University Press.

Coyne, I. (2009) Research with children and young people: the issues of parental (proxy) consent, *Children and Society*, 24: 227–37.

Coyne, I. (2010) Accessing children as research participants: examining the role of gatekeepers, *Child: Health, Care and Development*, 36(4): 452–4.

Danby, S. and Farrell A. (2004) Accounting for young children's competence in education research: new perspectives on research ethics, *Australian Educational Researcher*, 31(3): 35–49.

Davis, J., Watson, N. and Cunningham-Burley, S. (2008) Disabled children, ethnography and unspoken understanding: the collaborative construction of diverse identities, in P. Christensen and A. James (eds) *Research with Children: Perspectives and Practice*. London: Routledge.

Department of Health (2004) *Getting the Right Start: The National Service Framework for Children, Young People and Maternity Services – Standards for Hospital Services*, London: The Stationery Office.

Department of Health (2005) *The Research and Governance Framework for Health and Social Care*. London: The Stationery Office.

Evans, D. and Norman, P. (2002) Improving pedestrian road safety among adolescents: an application of the theory of planned behaviour, in D. Rutter and L. Quine (eds) *Changing Health Behaviour Intervention and Research with Social Cognition Models*. Buckingham: Open University Press.

Fivush, R. (2002) The development of autobiographical memory, in H. Westcott, G. Davies and H. Bull (eds) *A Handbook of Psychological Research and Forensic Practice*. Chichester: Wiley.

Fraser, S., Lewis, V., Ding, S., Kellett, M. and Robinson, C. (eds) (2004) *Doing Research with Children and Young People*. London: Sage.

Fry, J. and Neff, R. (2009) Periodic prompts and reminders in health promotion and health behaviour interventions: systematic review, *Journal of Medical Internet Research*, 11(2): e16.

Hart, R. (1992) *Children's Participation: From Tokenism to Citizenship*. Innocenti Essays No. 4. Florence: UNICEF Innocenti Research Centre.

Hendrick, H. (1992) Children and childhood, *Refresh*, 15: 1–4.

Hill, M., Davis, J., Prout, A. and Tisdall, K. (2004) Moving the participation agenda forward, *Children and Society*, 18: 77–96.

Home Office (2007) *Achieving Best Evidence in Criminal Proceedings: Guidance on Interviewing Victims and Witnesses and Using Special Measures*. London: The Stationery Office.

John, M. (2003) *Children's Rights and Power: Charging Up for a New Century*. London: Jessica Kingsley.

Kilkelly, U. (2008) *Children's Rights in Ireland: Law, Policy and Practice*. Dublin: Tottel Publishing.

Koch, T. (1996) Representation of a hermeneutic inquiry in nursing: philosophy, rigour and representation, *Journal of Advanced Nursing*, 24: 174–84.

Lewis, V., Kellett, M., Robinson, C., Fraser, S. and Ding. S. (eds) (2004) *The Reality of Research with Children and Young People*. London: Sage.

Long, T. and Johnson, M. (2000) Rigour, reliability and validity in qualitative research, *Clinical Effectiveness in Nursing*, 4: 30–7.

Long, T. and Johnson, M. (2007) *Research Ethics in the Real World: Issues and Solutions for Health and Social Care*. Edinburgh: Elsevier Churchill Livingstone.

Murray, C. and Hallett, C. (2000) Young people's participation in decisions affecting their welfare, *Childhood*, 7(1): 11–25.

Oates, K. (2007) Can we believe what children tell us?, *Journal of Paediatrics and Child Health*, 43: 843–7.

Office of the Minister for Children and Youth Affairs (2010) *Ethical Review and Children's Research in Ireland*. Dublin: The Stationery Office.

Pezdek, K. and Hinz, T. (2002) The construction of false events in memory, in H. Westcott, G. Davies and H. Bull (eds) *A Handbook of Psychological Research and Forensic Practice*. Chichester: Wiley.

Punch, S. (2002) Research with children: the same or different from research with adults?, *Childhood*, 9(3): 321–41.

Redfern, M. (chair) (2001) *Report of the Royal Liverpool Children's Inquiry into Organ Retention*. London: The Stationery Office.

Rolfe, G. (2006) Validity, trustworthiness and rigour: quality and the idea of qualitative research, *Journal of Advanced Nursing*, 53(3): 304–10.

Runeson, I., Elander, G., Hermeren, G. and Kristensson-Hallstrom, I. (2000) Children's consent to treatment: using a scale to assess degrees of self-determination, *Pediatric Nursing*, 26(5): 16–22.

Stalker, K., Carpenter, J., Connors, C. and Phillips, R. (2004) Ethical issues in social research: difficulties encountered gaining access to children in hospital for research, *Child: Care, Health and Development*, 30(4): 377–83.

Sutton, J., Smith, P. and Swettenham, J. (2004) Social cognition and bullying: social inadequacy or skilled manipulation?, in V. Lewis, V. Kellet, C. Robinson, S. Fraser and S. Ding (eds) *The Reality of Research with Children and Young People*. London: Sage.

United Nations (1989) *United Nations Convention on the Rights of the Child*. Geneva: United Nations.

Vrij, A. (2002) Deception in children: a literature review and implications for children's testimony, in H. Westcott, G. Davies and R. Bull (eds) *A Handbook of Psychological Research and Forensic Practice*. Chichester: Wiley.

Index